Diamond Advanced Praise

The Diamond Advantage provides women in the competitive business environment an excellent strategic plan to excel in the workplace. The PRISM model, (Personal, Relationship, Intellectual, Spiritual and Master Professional) is an in-depth plan which includes an exercise in identifying core values and implementing a workable model to succeed both personally and professionally. Inspired by her personal story, the reader is enriched by sharing in her personal history of challenging beginnings as the daughter of an immigrant mother, her struggles balancing family and career, and her job disappointments where she so successfully reengineered a business that she unintentionally worked her way out of a job. Dr. Simone demonstrates that just as a diamond is refined under pressure, so is the successful woman who reaches her goals with intentionality while in the refiner's fire of the work world. Dr. Simone's model includes a Diamond Success Declaration, a practical plan where you learn to "promote yourself without losing yourself – on your terms."

Professor Paul Benchener, former Director, Executive MBA Program, Rider University

Dr. Heather Simone is a forthright, always prepared, strategically minded business professional with 15 years of experience in major financial services companies. In *The Diamond Advantage*, Dr. Simone offers a framework for career success by thinking through the present into the future. Using the acronym of PRISM to outline a lens for achieving success, Dr. Simone endeavors to disperse motivational light through a series of exercises intended to clarify goals and set a pathway forward.

Dr. Nancy DiTomaso, Distinguished Professor, Rutgers Business School—Newark and New Brunswick

Dr. Heather Simone brilliantly presents her Diamond Life Advantage Framework with supporting examples of transformational leadership and the benefits of a diverse corporate culture, highlighting the importance of aligning core values and beliefs with personal action to achieve one's authentic success. Dr. Simone's Fortune 100 success story underscores the persistent drive and pressure one must withstand to achieve next level success. This dedicated climb, especially coming from a woman of color in the corporate 100 space, is a perfect analogy to the pressure a diamond must withstand to reveal its unique luminescent beauty. I couldn't help but sing "Shine on you crazy diamond" throughout this book as Dr. Simone encourages leaders, rising stars, and entrepreneurs to strategically plan their unique path to success. As an executive coach myself, having navigated similar corporate climates and entrepreneurial endeavors, I stand with Dr. Simone to say shine on and share your unique magnificence with the world. The world needs you. Whether you are a leader climbing the corporate ladder or an entrepreneur reaching for that next level, Dr. Simone encourages you to build your brand in every interaction - your success depends on it. Thank you Dr. Simone for courageously sharing your radiant brilliance.

I feel you are a role model for corporate leaders, rising stars and entrepreneurs especially for women of color being a woman of color yourself who has forged that path in a mostly white male business world. This makes you a more significant role model for other women of color who wish to shine brightly in their lives as well! Good for you!!! We need more successful women standing up for younger women. Wishing you even more success as you step out fully with your book! Congratulations!

Donna Karaba, Executive Coach, Bestselling Author, *Passion, Purpose, Profit: 9 Keys to Building an Authentic Executive Coaching Business*

This book was a real eye opener! There's nothing wrong with anyone trying to elevate themselves to where you want to be. Dr. Simone lays it all out for you, if you are willing to acknowledge your worth. As the book says, "Your value doesn't decrease based on someone's inability to see your worth." Loved it!

A. Murray, Business Executive

Wow! *The Diamond Advantage* speaks to anyone trying to get to their next level! It clearly provides a holistic view to success. I now have a plan forward. This is a MUST read!

B. Ogunnoiki, Business Leader

I was both excited and proud to read your book - *The Diamond Advantage*. In the book, you tackle an often talked about topic (Personal Success) in a straight-forward, insightful manner while maintaining a truly personal touch that meant so much to me as the reader. Your research was extensive and your guidance very impactful! The use of a personal strategic plan added a tangible conclusion to all the important lessons in - The Diamond Advantage.

Please continue to Shine On! As you know, excellence is almost always brighter than we think.

Barry M. Pelletteri, Adjunct Professor, Executive MBA Program, Rider University

This is Dr. Heather's calling. Her purpose. Read this book...listen to her speak and you'll understand why. Not only is she a wealth of knowledge, she expresses it in a way that you can't help but internalize her message. I have so much admiration for her positive spirit and her ability to use practical tools to make all the difference in the world!

Sandra Rodriguez Bicknell, Founder,
Cuts of a Diamond Coaching

The Diamond Advantage is a must read, start off right by reading *The Diamond Advantage* by Dr. Heather Simone!!! With leadership and research Dr. Heather Simone guides your journey with customized strategies for your success. As a business owner, *The Diamond Advantage* has totally changed my perspective in what it takes to live beyond my current expectations. I now have a better work- life approach in obtaining my success! Dr. Heather delivered her concepts supportively and genuinely, like a true friend. I will revisit this book time and time again! I highly recommend and will be sharing with my staff!

Janice Collins RN, WHNP -BC, Executive
Director, Collins Family Planning Clinic
janicecollins@collinsclinic.org

Being a business woman who came to this country as a Medical Dr. from the Ukraine I was extremely impressed with Dr. Heather Simone brilliant work 'The Diamond Advantage'. This book is one that I wish was written 25 years ago when I first arrived to America. The way Dr. Simone lays out many of the pitfalls women run into in business and how to resolve those issues effectively to a mutually successful conclusion is a must read for every small business owner, men included! The examples put forth are inspiring because they are true and from the real world perspective that Dr. Simone actually lived through. Through the pressure and ups and downs she came through stronger than ever. Built a career that any small to medium business owner would be envious of and would love to emulate. This book has given me a road map to continue to build my business and my brand no matter what road blocks are still put in front of us. I think we are in agreement that the disparity from a powerful women to a powerful man is slowly getting better and with Dr. Simone providing material like this we will continue to raise the bar.

Dr. Ledi Carpena, Owner, Golden Pair Clinic & Institute for Permanent and Corrective Cosmetics

I have to tell you, this is my 2 1/2 times reading this book. Each time I've discovered a new level of insight on my potential and how for so long, I've short-changed my success for one minor reason or another. The delivery of these principles is simply impeccable! I'm sooo uber proud of Dr. Heather and thank her for allowing me to share a small ray of love on this work that will serve the masses!!

The Diamond Advantage is a powerful breath of fresh air! Whether you are a just beginning your career, experienced some success, or you›re preparing to embark on your next phase success, you will appreciate the author for this roadmap! The PRISM framework is designed to help you to do the inside-work, simple. By doing so, you will have discovered precisely how to maximize your FULLEST potential! Personally, this read has ignited a new SPARK of courage - and I feel UNSTOPPABLE!

Dayna Marie, Entrepreneur,
UpscaleFinancialAgency.com

The Diamond Advantage

The DIAMOND Advantage

PROMOTE YOURSELF WITHOUT LOSING WHO YOU ARE

DR. HEATHER SIMONE

NEW YORK

LONDON • NASHVILLE • MELBOURNE • VANCOUVER

The Diamond Advantage

Promote Yourself Without Losing Who You Are

Published in New York, New York, by Morgan James Publishing in partnership with Difference Press. Morgan James is a trademark of Morgan James, LLC.
www.MorganJamesPublishing.com

ISBN 9781642794205 paperback
ISBN 9781642795295 audio
ISBN 9781642794212 eBook
Library of Congress Control Number: 2018968000

Cover Design by:
Christopher Kirk
www.GFSstudio.com

Interior Design by:
Chris Treccani
www.3dogcreative.net

Morgan James is a proud partner of Habitat for Humanity Peninsula and Greater Williamsburg. Partners in building since 2006.

Get involved today! Visit
MorganJamesPublishing.com/giving-back

Diamond Dedication

To my beloved mother, who poured into me from the very beginning and lovingly inspired me for next level success even when it seemed impossible.

Table of Contents

Introduction   *xvii*

Chapter 1:   Unprecedented Excellence is Within Reach
              ~ Journey to Personal Brilliance   1

Chapter 2:   My Story is Your Story ~
              In Looking for Diamonds,
              One May Overlook the Pearls   13

Chapter 3:   Brilliance Shines Brighter Together   25

Chapter 4:   Cut, Color, Clarity …Confidence   41

Chapter 5:   Intentional Relational   67

Chapter 6:   Intellectually Curious, A
              Childlike Wonder   83

Chapter 7:   Connected to Source, An
               Indispensable Resource   95

Chapter 8:   Earned MPS, Master Professional
               Studies   109

Chapter 9:   A Luminous Decision Abounds   127

Chapter 10:   Not All Grandeur and Pomp   139

Acknowledgements   149
Thank You!   153
About the Author   155
References   157

Introduction

I left the meeting elated. It had been many years in the making, but finally I could actually see the possibility of next level success. I had just been told that my company's senior female executive, three levels up my current reporting line, had recommended me for our newly launched Women Initiative Development Program. This was a first-of-its-kind initiative put forth by the president of our division. The cohort was made up of individuals who were deemed to have the potential for greater scope of responsibility for one to two levels up from their current position. This was a yearlong mentorship, training, and development, in addition to the great opportunity to lead a complex business program. Only nine women leaders from across the business were selected for this highly-regarded and prestigious nod. But the truth of the matter is this selection, although humbling, was merely the beginning. The yearlong dedication to solving a complex business issue, the visibility to senior leadership, and the collaboration with the other high-caliber women were certainly exciting benefits. However, managing this while juggling an already daunting workload would be no easy feat, but somehow I was fueled by the thought of even being considered for such a prestigious opportunity. I felt accomplished, but had not arrived at my goal.

It was May and as most began to plan summer vacations and long lazy-hazy weekends to break from extended work weeks, I began to plan a strategy for the next couple of months. After all, isn't that how we solve all our issues? Create a strategy, right? This strategic plan, however, would have its unique challenges, as every plan does. What I know to be true is to expect to contend with surprises along the way with any intended plan, both professionally and personally. In other words, expect the unexpected. In this case, navigating the specific pressures of no longer having support staff was one thing in terms of increased workload; however, dealing with a reorganization added another level of complexity. Particularly, this reorganization repositioned a colleague (who somehow seemed to operate on opposing views as peers) to become my direct manager, and was entirely a professional dance for the elite and highly skilled at corporate culture dexterity. The transition from being peers to direct reports often is a challenge in itself. All this while leading a very visible process re-engineering implementation for the division, the newest high priority initiative. The truth of the matter is – I was certainly up for the challenge. Opportunities like these rarely align in this fashion. To be highly thought of was one thing, but to be tapped on the shoulder again for a future opportunity of this scope, likely had the same probability of lighting striking in the same place twice.

As the day turned to the afternoon, I grew with excitement to share with my tribe, my family. My husband, teenage boys, mother, and siblings had lived through my competitive edge, type A, high-achiever syndrome for as far back as I can remember. They had been my stealth supporters who readily moved obstacles out of the way, who not only wiped my tears during times of difficulty but had also cried with me, and had waved pom-poms high as my biggest cheerleaders during some of those proudest moments. I am because they are. I can recall numerous vacation cruises where I would have my laptop on the beach writing papers for graduate school. I called it the mobile office. The boys would be frolicking in the ocean with their new snorkeling gear as I typed away. "Mom, did you see us?" they would call out. "Yes, I saw you, nice!" Sometimes I would respond without looking up from the mobile office. My heart breaks even thinking about how many more of those types of moments were needed to get through this next phase. An internal tension existed where I was energized about the challenges of obtaining next level success; however, the relationship costs were taxing. The guilt of feeling invigorated by the challenges knowing that the other responsibilities, as a wife, mother, daughter, sister, would inevitably be impacted. No excuses, push through, I told myself. My solace was in the notion that next level success was not only for me, but for them – my tribe. I worked hard so that they wouldn't have to. I was fully committed to up-front sacrifice for long-term gain. Investments made today would have dividend gains in the future. #pressure-makes-diamonds

Indeed the summer months were challenging. No longer in school, my primary focus was to re-engineer the division's governance process. During prior years of supporting the convoluted process, I'd taken copious notes on design thinking concepts to reduce unnecessary complexity and had shared with management that if the opportunity ever presented itself, here were ideas of how to streamline the process, saving time, making the practice more dynamic and iterative, and ultimately increasing ease of use from a user perspective – in essence, efficiencies abounded. As an extension of my role and responsibility, I was charged to lead the implementation of those ideas I had presented. As the Divisional Director of Strategic Planning, each of the twenty functional areas submitted their respective strategic plan that aligned with the overall strategy. Leading the division through the change management process, as with any transformation, was far easier on paper. Getting senior leadership buy-in and organizational adoption took time and a great deal of collaboration and effort. Being short-staffed and upgrading processes from Microsoft Word to Excel software added additional complexities to the already compressed timeline. Many summer nights were spent analyzing extracted data to identify trends. On a number of occasions, data quality was detected as subpar and revisions were needed. Similar to prior experiences, I took diligent notes for opportunities of improvement in the next iteration of the process. In one instance, in re-checking prepared pre-read materials the night before a preliminary management report meeting, I offered to make the needed updates and resend the materials to the meeting participants. The offer was declined; it would be positioned as preliminary and further updates would follow. I met many challenges but overcame them as they emerged.

Summer turned to fall and the new process was implemented successfully. I felt accomplished. The entire division would be following a process that I designed and implemented. Maturing the process through lessons learned and feedback would be subsequent steps. As maturing the process was underway, new priorities, outside of my original expected scope of responsibilities, emerged. Optimistically, I assumed the less strategic tasks in hopes it would be a means to an end. As year-end approached, I began to reflect on the past couple of months and thought about a fresh start for the new year. Once I gathered my thoughts, I discussed them with my manager.

January of the following year, I had a regularly-scheduled meeting with my manager. I walked into the conference room and a Human Resource representative was waiting. Let's just say that's typically not a good sign. She shared that my job was being eliminated and that it had nothing to do with my performance. The organization was looking for efficiencies and I had done such a stellar job in re-engineering the governance process that my role was going to be reclassed to a lower level so that the work implemented would be sustained.

I wasn't angry. I was numb. How could I have possibly worked myself out of my own job? How could the organization reward "top talent identified for greater scope of responsibility" in this way? After all that I have given this organization through the years? Re-engineering the governance process barely scratched the surface. The numerous *extra* projects I took on such as being a panelist for employee affinity groups, facilitating organizational trainings, and founding a mentoring programing, just to name a few. At this point, I had far more questions than answers but at my core, I believe that everything – *everything* – good, bad, and ugly – happens for a reason. Before receiving this blindsiding news, I was feeling a need for a change, a desire for greater impact of next level success, but certainly didn't anticipate this. #Diamond-process-endures

About a month after I received the news, I still wasn't quite sure what direction I wanted to take. I had already completely transitioned my work and handed in my laptop. It was the last day I would have access to the company system via my cell phone. Sometime around 4 p.m. – 4:12, to be exact – an email came through on my mobile from the Chief Executive Office. It was the admin requesting a meeting on behalf of the C-level executive. The email stated that he had heard that there were organizational changes in my area and he wanted to schedule a meeting to discuss. I thought highly of this leader and knew he was fairly familiar with the standard of my work. Several years back, he had been the Executive Sponsor of a cross-functional program I was leading. Had he remembered – and taken the time to care? Extremely impressive considering the volume of information and number of competing priorities he managed as status quo. Due to his heavy international travel, the meeting was scheduled for more than a month out. Even if nothing came out of the meeting, I felt valued by this gesture that perhaps my work effort hadn't been in vain after all.

It was pouring down rain the day of the meeting. As the rain trickled on the windshield, it created a peaceful lull that allowed me to gather my thoughts. I had no particular agenda, or intention for negative talk – I was just open to dialogue of go-forward possibilities. Traffic was moving slower than usual but I was still tracking well for the 5:30 p.m. meeting. I arrived at the employee parking deck and waited behind a vehicle that seemed to be having issues with getting through security. After fifteen minutes or so of waiting behind the vehicle with emergency flashers on, I beckoned to the guard, who seemed to be on a long wait on the phone. I asked if he knew how much longer it would take to get into the deck because I didn't want to be late for my 5:30 p.m. meeting. He told me it would be best to enter at the other entrance, which would mean reversing into the oncoming traffic during rush hour. Although mortified I'd be rear-ended, I gave him a half smile and a simple thank you. After carefully making my way to the other entrance of the parking deck, I was pleased to see a familiar face. The attendant knew me by name and I gladly handed her my badge to swipe me in. The entire screen went red when she processed my badge. In that very moment I realized that the day before this meeting had technically been my official separation day in the system. I quickly apologized and handed her my driver's license to prevent any further undue delay. She said, "I can see a reservation was made for you but I do need to call." Long story short, she was required to confiscate my badge, I had to reverse out of that parking deck – again – but she was kind enough to ask the other attendant to watch my car outside of the parking facility while I ran (literally, in heels) up to my meeting, glistening a bit from being in the rain.

As I small talked with the admin in the elevator, telling her about my just-experienced adventure at the parking deck, we got off the lift and finished up the light conversation in front of her desk. Apparently, a portion of our conversation was overheard, as Mr. Executive himself appeared in the doorway of the corner office. He invited me over and I couldn't help but notice the immaculate views from the nearly floor-to-ceiling windows. Let's just say there are apartments in Manhattan smaller than his office. He offered me a seat in the couch area and a bottle of water. Clearly, he did overhear a bit of the conversation, because as he opened his bottle of water he apologized for how eventful parking had been that evening. I quickly dismissed the incident – it was nearly comical in hindsight – parking was the least of our challenges. I genuinely thanked him for even reaching out and taking time out of his schedule to meet with me. Gestures like these from someone at his level go a very long way and I didn't take it lightly. The engaging conversation seemed to quantum leap through time. It was evident he did his homework and knew I had a stellar year and a few of the highlights of my performance outcomes. He expressed perspectives about managing efficiencies and talent in parallel where the concepts are not mutually exclusive. Most importantly, if I was interested, he offered to use his influence to explore other roles within the organization. And just as I said yes in agreement, a junior grandfather clock struck the hour of six o'clock. I turned toward the direction of the clock to verify I really heard what I thought I heard. He laughed. "Yes, it's a grandfather clock," as if he read my mind. "One of the best gifts I've received. It keeps all my meetings on track."

"I can see why," I replied. We agreed to keep in touch and that it had been a great meeting. I had some decisions to make.

Success is not final~
Failure is not fatal~
It is the courage that counts.
— **WINSTON CHURCHILL**

Chapter 1:

Unprecedented Excellence is Within Reach ~ Journey to Personal Brilliance

---

The success journey for each of us~
is unique as a precious diamond that forms over time ~
through stimulating, yet disruptive environments~
that ultimately radiates a brilliance that luminates
unprecedented excellence.
– DR. HEATHER SIMONE

Unprecedented excellence is our personal success, the essence of what we strive for. Reaching unprecedented excellence would yield satisfaction and purpose at the peak levels of the success journey. Personal impact at that level will not only be meaningful, but also rewarding. The true arrival. Success is in fact a journey made up of countless choices and decisions, both large and small, that etch definition in our path as goals are redefined when targeted achievements are accomplished. Costs and consequences are inevitably a byproduct of this virtuous cycle. This is particularly true for women, who often contend with needing to prove themselves professionally with credentials and/or experience that exceeds their male colleagues. All too often, extra credentials at work are needed to be 'equitable' while assuming the majority share of household and family responsibilities at home. This is an unfortunate harsh reality that recent grassroots efforts have propelled to the national stage, but if you keep your focus finite, and engage in candid discussions with like-minded hearts and minds, I'm confident that you will have clarity and significance about your next level success decision, without losing yourself or the quality of the relationships that are important to you. You can have it all.

I'm energized to go on this success journey with you and excited for your success promotion. My own success paradigm calls for me to help others define their success. It is through my own reflections, revelations, and in serving others that I share insight to develop a customized approach to promoting yourself without losing yourself or what matters to you the most. For that reason, our connection is not from happenstance or mere luck. According to Google, luck is defined as "success or failure apparently brought by chance rather than through one's own actions." Your actions are of a higher order that is more purposeful than a fluke. In the same way that we became connected, others will recognize the clarity in you. Welcome to your success journey that will promote you to next level success with significance and meaning that aligns to what and who matters to you the most.

I've developed The Diamond Advantage model through cases that I've coached, and high-performing teams I've developed to new standards of excellence, academic research at the doctoral level, and insight gained through the world-class coaching that I've received to manage my own personal and professional success journey. The Diamond Advantage utilizes a customized approach that reflects your unique cut, color, and clarity core values to ensure an idyllic fit. The proven framework explores five dimensions to unprecedented and streamlined success through the PRISM approach. This signature approach delves into the specific domains of Personal, Relationships, Intellectual, Spiritual, and Master Professional areas of your life to create your specific masterpiece plan that unambiguously aligns with your Diamond Blueprint. Yes, the five areas are few but the results profound. This comprehensive model will allow you to achieve your success goals and have it all! Rest assured friend, you're not alone in your concern, nor will you be in your success journey. You are the owner of your success, and this book experience will serve as a guide to your radiating brilliance.

The diamond, more than a billion years old, is the hardest natural substance on earth.[1]

Likewise, it's brilliant, glamorous, breathtaking, and mysterious. There's a wealth of history and knowledge surrounding the popular gem, an uncanny but necessary journey that results in an extraordinary product that is worth the unconventional arrival. Who would imagine that under radical temperatures of approximately 2,000°F and extreme pressures of being thrust from volcanic activity from nearly one hundred miles beneath the earth's surface would result in such an unapologetic, noteworthy outcome? An outcome that exudes strength – with a hardiness that only another diamond can cut; and with a noteworthy beauty, as evidenced by the global demand from consumers worldwide. Clearly, no two precious stones would assume the same path to emerge from the earth's surface, and further, no two are alike, as each piece represents a sole and exclusive stance.

Similarly, our success journey is akin to nature due to the dynamic complexity as a number of factors are involved in the evolving trek. Nature, however, has an advantage as it instinctively reacts to chemical reactions, intense pressures, and high temperature combinations, where *discernment* in our case can introduce a lack of confidence or uncertainty as decisions, particularly regarding career and success progression, are rendered. There are macro and micro influences, vague nuances, and unexpected shocks that change the intended direction. There is an ongoing reassessment that needs to occur to comprehensively consider all inputs and indicators. Because each of us is unique, each path will also have inherent individual distinction. Due to the complexity of understanding the influencers, unwritten rules coupled with the passion to succeed can at times seem overwhelming. Success is a challenging path that comes with failures and lessons learned, and takes hard work, dedication, and disruptive growth to thrust us forward, while tapping into resources and developing networks, as well as assessing costs and consequences as decisions are made along the way. The journey is an aggregate of decisions and the actions that follow to move closer to a desired goal. The lack of a decision and inaction can also yield results that can potentially impact success. I'm all too familiar with the multifaceted nature of the complex paradigm.

A brilliant is a modern round cut diamond that consists of a scattering of fifty-eight facets reflecting exceptional brilliance.[2]

The multifaceted nature driving your success for so long has been primarily and logically your smarts, expertise, and intellect – your head. You've done all the right things to prepare – attended the right school, were an exemplary student with the grades and extracurriculars, interned at a great organization, landed "the" job, and have now worked your way up the corporate ladder, where you've earned the respect of your peers but still have fire in your belly for something more. You're almost afraid to utter your aspirations and concerns to others outside of your trusted tribe because by some accounts, there should be no concern. From the outside, it's a great life. However, your inner circle is well aware of the dichotomy. The multifaceted piece – the head versus heart issue – is where the tension lies. Seeking next level success so that you could find greater personal satisfaction, meaning, and significance would come at a cost. You are likely excited and a bit thrilled by the thought of the challenge, yet fearful of losing yourself in overwhelm and worse, losing the quality of the relationships of your core circle. Missing out on your important events, milestones, firsts, lasts, and in-betweens – memories that would be forever gone – or those just-because moments that turn out to be so special, spent either silently holding hands or having hearty belly-laughs that gives you stitches in your side.

I can recall a close friend, a high achiever who happens to have a role reversal arrangement in her household. She was former military, top in her field, and her husband was a stay at home dad. I listened attentively as she shared her story one day over tea. Her eyes welled with tears as she explained that she finally made it to one of her daughter's parent-teacher conferences. She was late and rushed into the classroom just as the teacher was completing her positive report on their daughter. She said she was proud to see her daughter growing up so fast, but somehow I knew there was more behind the emotion in her eyes than she cared to discuss. It seemed her heart was giving her a nudge, perhaps from a level of guilt. Certainly the arrangement worked for them on paper, but the demands of the job often kept her one step behind the family connection.

The multifaceted aspect of the head and heart, despite even the best of emotional intelligence, eventually connects. The intellect may lead, but the emotion will eventually follow. Because there are a myriad of ways to pursue an individual success path, the mind is agile in problem solving as decision making is narrowed and influencers shift direction; however, the path generally proceeds forward – with minor ebbs and flows along the way. In spite of powering forward, it can be draining, even daunting, from an emotional perspective. As a comparison, the stock market consistently has peaks and valleys as it trades daily but historically, when assessed over long-term time horizons, it inevitably increases. Although historical evidence is not indicative of future performance, some investors are not comfortable with the market fluctuations and opt for more conservative risk tolerances. An individual's risk tolerances, similarly, are largely tied to personal emotion. In theory, it would be ideal to maximize returns but not at the risk of an equal and opposite downturn. Without risk, there is no reward. Are you willing to bank on *you* and make an investment in yourself? Take it from one who knows based on my own experiences, from my heart to yours, it's not unusual to want the desires of both the head and the heart – they are ultimately connected. A sage once said, "Search in your heart with your intellect to find the answers." Multifaceted indeed.

Clouds in Stones Perspectives ~ Diamond crystals and clouds are essentially just tiny diamonds that were trapped within the larger diamond crystal as it formed, [...] clouds of pinpoint size diamond crystals that resemble constellations of stars up in the sky, they sparkle and twinkle just like stars. [3]

Who is establishing your great expectation? Before we begin our journey into your next level success – where clarity will come into crystal clear focus, where purpose and significance will align with what matters to you the most, all while embracing dear relationships – first let's level on who exactly is establishing your great expectation. We agree the end goal is ultimately integration of prioritizing key moments of work and professional experiences that will allow a demanding but orderly cadence to your eventful life. Orderly, not chaotic; contained, not running rampant; and most importantly, a promotion that aligns and is meaningful to your exclusive Diamond Blueprint. Yes, having it all.

Prior to beginning this compelling and effective work that will require reflection, assessment, and accountability, a disruptive transformation is a prerequisite to the fulfilling reward. Let's genuinely consider: who is establishing your great expectation? Pause here for a moment to avoid a knee-jerk reaction. Take a breath and know this is coming from a place of benevolence. Let's take another breath and reflect. Are you pursuing *your* dream or someone else's? Is this an expectation for yourself or one that was placed on you a long time ago that you're still working on from a loved one – perhaps a parent or spouse? Or, was a teacher, guidance counselor, or coach trying to be helpful but you've evolved since then? A manager? Or was it someone along the way that said you couldn't do something and you're secretly proving them wrong? Take as long as you need as you reflect. Once you have that answer, do you still agree with the success definition? If not, revise your success dream come true. It's fine that all the details are not in place, we'll get there. It's important that you can begin to visualize yourself at your next level of success. As you take the success journey, the details will emerge, and any anxiety or fear will likely dissipate into passion and excitement for what lies ahead.

Now, we've discussed that the success journey is multifaceted, head and heart connected, and made up of a series of decisions. The question: who is establishing your great expectation? We've learned to search in our heart with our intellect to find the answer. This was the first decision of the success journey – *to recognize and realize that you are the owner of your success and you establish your own great expectation*. Congratulations. This decision you've just made demonstrates authority regardless of *how* the success paradigm was received, whether by a parent, friend, or otherwise. You've owned it. It's entirely your decision. With that said, as success owner you are the beneficiary of the decision, which also means that you're accountable and will course correct when needed. Relish in your new beginning.

I'm delighted that you've made the first decision to be the owner of your success and set your own expectations in your success journey! Notice that the previous reflection considered *how* the success paradigm was given to you, suggesting "by way of" or "a means," not your *why*, which is a very different question. Later in our journey we'll discuss "the why" in more detail, but for now, it's important to highlight the difference. The motivation, or *why*, for your success journey should energize you and typically have connection to something other than you as an individual. It should feel purposeful. The *how*, on the other hand, has more to do with the conduit through which the concept or success idea was given to you. With that transparency set, it's important to remember that *your value doesn't decrease based on someone's inability to see your worth.*

In other words, I recognize that you are deserving of a promotion and that it has been many years in the making. I also realize that you have sacrificed both time and relationships and even maneuvered with limited resources to work toward the end goal. The tribe has been on board for years. I appreciate what you bring to the table and the value you contribute to your organization consistently while others, who don't seem to put in half the amount of effort and proven work ethic that you do, have been recognized. You are more than a solid team player, you're a top performer. In fact, for the last several years you've been struggling with how to dim your light so that others could shine. I certainly give you credit for wanting to hold space for others to achieve, but *your value doesn't decrease based on someone's inability to see your worth.* Further, as you hold space for others to achieve, ensure it is not at the expense at reaching your own fullest potential. Your next level success should be grounded in your inner motivation and desires and not on proving or disproving outside forces' validation.

You are deserving of next level success, and I will hold space for you on this success journey, as we take this success journey together.

I look forward to you stepping assuredly into your personal brilliance. Your unparalleled success awaits.

Chapter 2:

My Story is Your Story – In Looking for Diamonds, One May Overlook the Pearls

---

Early Day Impressions

I vividly recall those dreadful mornings getting up for preschool. It was always dark and seemingly before the rest of the world rose for the day. My mother ran the morning routine like clockwork. Every morning my lightly-brewed hot tea and grilled cheese sandwich waited on the stove; teacup on stove, covered by a saucer plate, which served to keep the liquids warm and house the grilled cheese sandwich, then covered by another saucer plate. Genius. To this day I still have a hot cup of coffee or tea to start my day.

On this particular day, the morning routine became a particular challenge due to the frigid temperatures and light falling snow. I thought to myself, as any five- or six-year-old would, "How on earth are we going to make it across town in the snow?" As a child, I wasn't quite sure how long it took us every morning, but I knew we took two of the big buses and I slept most of the way. I did try to stay awake while waiting for the bus, but oftentimes I would doze off standing up, face snuggled into my mother's mid-section with Mom's loving arm around me. This morning journey from our first floor Brooklyn apartment in Canarsie, just outside of Brownsville, to the Marine Park section by public transportation was the only thing I knew. Mom did have her driver's license, but she didn't drive and we didn't own a car. So, every morning we got up early to take the two buses to my school and then she boarded her train to Manhattan to work at a large hotel. For me, education was a non-negotiable from the very beginning. It was the opportunity my mom never had as an immigrant single mother of three. If that meant taking a daily trek into the "other neighborhood" to get a better education, that's what we were going to do – and this morning was no different.

I followed her lead, and watched as she took out my fuchsia-colored snow suit and coordinating boots from the front closet. Concern turned to excitement as I was now eager to face the weather in a fashionable ensemble of my favorite color! The heavy boots, the belt, and the drawstring hood that pulled tight for the munchkin look somehow mentally equipped me to enthusiastically face the challenges of the day. Outside waiting for the bus that morning, my eyes teared as the wind brisked by. Mom quickly wiped the single tear as it fell from my eyes. "I'm cold," I mumbled. She responded, "The bus doesn't come to our neighborhood and we have to get you there so you'll have a good education and no one will walk over you. Just imagine you're on the beach and it's not cold at all." Imagine; I did. I started to imagine and dream big dreams.

> *What you think, you become~*
> *What you feel, you attract~*
> *What you imagine, you create.*
> — BUDDHA

Getting home from preschool was as equally challenging. Since the bus didn't go to our neighborhood, my older brother was assigned to pick me up from school daily. He quickly became tired of the commute and often "forgot" to get me. Thinking back now, I assume going into other communities in the 1980s where he might not always feel welcome played a part in his forgetfulness. As the only person of color in my school, I stood out for regularly being the last student left at the school. I didn't realize that I was any different from any of the other students; the teachers and students alike were all very kind to me. I have fond memories of those days. On this day in particular, it began to get dark and no one came to get me. I waited outside the principal's office, coloring in a coloring book with a sixty-four pack of Crayola crayons. I would outline the figure boldly and then shade it in using the crayons with fancy names. The principal then appeared outside of the office. He said that it was getting late and I must be hungry. He said he had just spoken with my mother and she was on her way but would pick me up from his home. I was puzzled and began to get nervous because Mom didn't want me to go to anyone's house. Although I don't recall the principal's name, I do recall that I trusted him. He had a slim build, glasses, and always wore a kippah.

My nervousness dissipated when we were greeted at his front door by his wife and two daughters, who were around my age. We ate and just as we began to play, Mom showed up in a cab. I could see that she was embarrassed and a bit irritated, and she apologized profusely. There was no loud shouting or angry voices. I waved goodbye to my new friends and skipped away to the taxi that waited outside. But things did change that day. From that day on, Mom arranged for a taxi to pick me up from school daily and drive me home across town. I can still recall my heartbeat pounding in my ears each time I reached for the rear taxi door handle, terrified to get in the back seat. This certainly would have been unheard of today and thankfully I got through that period unscathed. Little did I know that walking through fear in the preschool days was preparation for the disruptive climates that lay ahead.

Later Years

Not only was I first-generation American from immigrant parents, I was also one of the first in my family to go to college. Although I was accepted to top schools based on academic performance, I ended up going my state university to defray costs. Being one of the first to attend college had its challenges in navigating the process, particularly on limited resources. Being on the pre-medical track called for numerous natural science, mathematics, and chemistry courses, and there was a bit of art to taking them in the right combination to avoid overload. Although I consistently had a job from age fourteen and dabbled in cheerleading and track, as well as other civic organizations, I had a maniacal focus on success and became diligent about planning my time. A few friends didn't work at all and their only jobs were to study and excel in school. Although I worked, I still recall instances where I was sitting for mid-year exams and did not have the textbook yet. Science textbooks were easily five hundred dollars or more, so I spent many hours in the library reading and copying information I needed from the course textbook. The medical doctor goals were sidetracked when I ended up getting married, having an infant, and a toddler by undergraduate graduation. I had a baby over spring break and was back in class a week and a half later pursuing my goals, unwavering from my focus. My sheltered life in Brooklyn left my discernment in choosing a life partner largely underdeveloped, so my tumultuous and short-lived marriage ended abruptly. Now with a young family, I decided to double down on driving to success.

My first real job was in financial services in a Fortune 50 investment firm. I attempted to get a job in the medical field but to no avail due to lack of experience. This is where I unintentionally started in the industry where I have remained ever since. This industry selection was perhaps an unintentional choice, but all part of a greater plan working in my favor. I went with the flow and trusted it without deviating. I may not have chosen my professional field outright, but it chose me. Working at the investment firm changed the trajectory of my career as my quest to learn the business was just as great as my passion to build a book of business. Dinner table talks at my house weren't about calls, puts, or margin investment strategies. I became licensed and began to acquire a sizable book of business. I recall a defining moment, still in the office around 9:00 p.m., when I looked up at the time. I didn't realize it was that late as I was engrossed in work and time had gotten away from me. My tribe was, of course, caring for my young ones, but yet another occasion passed where they would have gone to bed by the time I got home. The tears streamed down my face uncontrollably. It was time for me to call it a day.

The Climb

Several years later, I successfully completed a management trainee program at a prominent retail bank. Repeatedly, I would turn around non-performing banking centers to breakthrough performance in sales and operations while mitigating risks. Leadership quickly realized the value potential and reassigned me to the next non-performing center so that I could apply my successful methods there as well. I excelled at managing teams and developing strategies to solve complex business issues. The digital product age was upon us and I also became involved in its approaches and development. Soon afterwards, I was promoted to vice president and had the opportunity to manage multiple retail banking centers, splitting my time accordingly. Through candid conversations with leadership, it was recommended I obtain my graduate degree and shadow regional management for a year to prepare for the next level. The next level success was to manage a group of eight to ten banking centers. I was fully committed to the outlined plan and stayed late whenever necessary, and showed up on random Saturdays to ensure the efficiency and optimization of each center. Several reorganizations and mergers with two other institutions resulted in shifts in leadership. At this point, I had shadowed as suggested for ten months and enrolled in an all-day Saturday graduate program. The choice of schools in my selection process was limited to Saturday programs, to be the least disruptive to my work week.

When my company switched to new leadership, I decided to provide a detailed update on my previously-discussed career plan and approach. To my surprise, the new leadership team was not aware of the development recommendations or an advocate for the absence of VP presence in the centers on Saturdays. I calmly and confidently assured the leadership team of the competence of my team and provided examples of their performance under the guidance of my assistant manager. Further, I had paid for the upcoming semester as discussed in prior leadership conversations and was in jeopardy to losing the funds already committed. To no avail; I did not get the approval to proceed as planned. Leadership, let's call her Alice, recommended that I revise my plan to include online graduate learning as opposed to an in-classroom setting, although Alice completed most of her education at an Ivy League university. I was devastated to say the least, because I knew the time for any tuition fund reimbursements had expired. I absolutely wanted next level success, but at what cost and under what terms? I was in a predicament and had to make the toughest business decision of my life. I was on a great trajectory to next level success that seemed to be disrupted by an uncontrollable challenge that presented itself.

This was a family decision. My tribe, no doubt, would be impacted either way. I went home that evening, feeling defeated that all I did was follow the guidance and instructions provided to me, committed time and resources to my decision, only to be told to shift my approach. The issue was that I was already financially and personally committed. I broached the conversation with my husband, by then of numerous years, who told me that I had his support either way but that it sounded like it was time to move on from my current position. Somehow, I already knew the answer before the discussion began. There was no doubt that next level success was still my desire; however, my approach would need to shift. The following day, I submitted my resignation to my organization in order to pursue my graduate education. It was an investment in myself to better prepare for future roles. I was unemployed and a bit unsure, but willing to take a calculated risk, not knowing exactly how it would materialize.

I walked through the fear, mustered the courage to be grateful for the challenge that Alice presented to me, and pushed through the disruptive and challenging environment to get on the other side. Once the announcement was shared broadly, leaders and colleagues alike provided me with an unexpected outpouring of genuine well wishes and accolades that was beyond measure. I was so enthralled with delivering on expectations that I had not realized how many were impacted by my actions, established model, and drive – and were quietly cheering me on. Funny, in my next job (which took me over a year to land due to a down market), I quickly established a mentorship with a high-level female executive. I recall that in one discussion with my mentor, she casually asked me if I knew an Alice. When I acknowledged that I had a former boss by that name, she said, "She's been asking me about you and your well-being." They ran in the same circles! My mentor, who I respected and adored, then said, "Alice has sent a message for you: 'Let me know if this new organization isn't treating you right, we may be able to find you an opportunity over here.'" Pushing through, even when riddled with fear and self-doubt, gives you the chance to recover. To be immobilized with inaction guarantees one thing; it assures that things will remain the same. The Universe sent me a message through my mentor. It. Is. Well. It was years later, at my subsequent employer, that the experience shared at the opening of this book occurred and I left my meeting elated.

Our deepest fear
is not that we are inadequate~
Our deepest fear
is that we are powerful beyond measure~
It is our light, not our darkness
that most frightens us~
We ask ourselves,
Who am I to be brilliant, gorgeous, talented, fabulous?
Actually, who are you not to be?
You playing small does not serve the world~
We are all meant to shine~
It's not just in some of us;
it's in all of us~
And as we let our own light shine,
we unconsciously give others
permission to do the same.
— MARIANNE WILLIAMSON

Success is not final~
Failure is not fatal~
It is the courage that counts.
— WINSTON CHURCHILL

Chapter 3:

Brilliance Shines Brighter Together

If you want to go fast,
Go alone~
If you want to go far,
Go together.
— **African Proverb**

We've established that unprecedented excellence is our personal success. We recognize that it is a dynamic, multifaceted journey that you've committed many years of hard work, dedication, and resources to pursue. Most importantly, we acknowledge that you have not walked this journey alone. Thankfully, your tribe has been with you along the way through the good and turbulent times when resources were limited. And now comes the emerging news that many, women and others, including myself, have experienced similar journeys to yours and there is strength in numbers. Like a unique gem, our distinct and disruptive paths were an awakening that gently guided to greater level of consciousness to a better you, your next level success defined to custom fit your exclusive essence. Friend, you should feel elated and relieved that next level success is certainly attainable without losing the relationships that matter the most and that our engagement together will outline the steps to achieve your distinct success that will align to your personal values. This solution, called The Diamond Advantage, is a powerful journey proven to promote yourself without losing yourself by navigating the complex process of additional scope, responsibility, and commitment that next level success naturally brings through compelling personal stories, research, and insightful exercises. These collective tailored strategies from each of the PRISM domains – namely, the Personal, Relationships, Intellectual, Spiritual, and Master Professional areas of your life – will bring clarity, meaning, and significance to individual success paradigms by integrating professional and personal aims. This experience will take care to review each domain, one by one, and delve into your preferences within each. This will result in revealing your tailored strategic plan to get to your next level of success. In sum, you will have it all, based on your terms, creating space for your personal brilliance to radiate with unprecedented excellence.

Indeed, this is great news. This categorical shift is material and, as alluded prior, this process is disruptive, but well worth the desired outcome.

> *Growth begins~*
> *at the end of your comfort zone.*
> **– ADAPTED FROM NEALE DONALD WALSCH.**

I trust that it's reassuring to know that I am here with you every step of the way, not silently cheering you on, but overtly and openly advocating for your success. As we stretch through your growth zone, know that your customized success, which considers both professional and personal objectives, is the ultimate goal. This will require reflection and realization before your reward is identified. So, before we begin The Diamond Advantage journey, I'll share that my own success equation calls for this partnership with you. Through my own success, ambition, and self-discoveries, sharing insights to facilitate achievement in others is what manifolds significance and purpose in my success paradigm. In other words, I recognize the prominence of our partnership in being entrusted to guide you through facets of head and heart insights to reach your desired outcomes. I will provide tips and direction to guide your process, and your thoughtful reflection during this experience will determine your personalized success strategy. I look forward to celebrating your redefined success.

The Diamond Advantage

I coined The Diamond Advantage as *the* solution to determine next level success with clarity and significance that aligns with individual core values and strengths. Through the PRISM framework the five-dimensional model for success includes aspects of Personal, Relationships, Intellectual, Spiritual, and Master Professional. The Personal domain explores the personal aspects of what makes you uniquely different, your strengths, core values, and preferences. The Relationships domain identifies the categories of your relationships and discusses the meaning of each in your life. The Intellectual domain delves into the importance of consistently learning, even in non-traditional ways and how this positively influences other areas of your life. The Spiritual domain turns inward to review the beliefs that serve as an internal compass that guides decision making and actions. Finally, the Master Professional is the area that represents your professional life. This domain is typically where most of us focus for next level success, however the exploration in the other areas will provide insight in how to up-level professional success. This framework will guide you through the complexities of personal and professional insights to navigate and seamlessly integrate a refined accomplished future for you with fresh perspective. The success journey is an ongoing process; as such, this model equips you with appropriate tools as your priorities evolve. I developed this critical insight through personal experiences, client testimonies, research, and perception exercises that align personal and professional aims with customized core principles that uniquely result in tailored and redefined next level success that honors valued relationships without losing yourself. This journey will result in you having a specific actionable plan to achieve your next level success.

Anxiousness and trepidation dissipate and clarity, meaning, and significance become prevalent as you journey through this program. Upon completion of this experience, you will have a newly found clarity about your next level success and an action plan to get you to your desired goals. You can expect your actions and behaviors to be expressed more confidently due to your improved alignment to meaning and increased level of transparency. Integration of success across the five domains will be evident as they seamlessly impact one another. Regardless of industry or sector, the effects are the same: promotion to an improved success paradigm that allows for your unparalleled excellence to radiate.

> *The success journey for each of us~*
> *is unique as a precious diamond that forms over time ~*
> *through stimulating, yet disruptive environments~*
> *that ultimately radiates a brilliance that luminates*
> *unprecedented excellence.*
> – DR. HEATHER SIMONE

Just like each diamond's creation is unique, each success journey has its unique disruptive path to definitive brilliance as no two roads to success are exactly alike. Also similar to nature, we each have a distinguishing competitive advantage that sets us apart from others as no two gems are alike. I am in awe even trying to comprehend the magnitude of randomness in the endless possibilities of individual brilliance. Through challenges, both personal and professional, we learn through stimulating but disruptive teaching moments that stretch us beyond our comfort zones. It is at the edge of our comfort zones that next level success is up-leveled. The more comfortable we get being uncomfortable, the more we embrace reimagined possibilities.

The five-dimensional model for success includes a holistic consideration of one's full identity to authentically determine core values and inherent strengths. This comprehensive approach is exemplary to other singular aspect approaches. Overlooking parts of who we are would inaccurately depict natural tendencies and preferences, jeopardizing maturing to the fullest success potential. As I previously described, the PRISM framework consists of Personal, Relationships, Intellectual, Spiritual, and Master Professional, with each dimension as its own discrete category; however, connections across the dimensions exist as changes in any dimension will have impacts on other areas, both negatively and positively. For example, when I was a college student with an unclear understanding of the ramifications of credit card debt, on a campus that regularly offered free gifts outside of the library, cafeteria, and almost every other major campus building, it was no surprise that I ended up with seven credit cards by graduation. The burden of high credit card debt impacted the financial dimension of my framework negatively, putting stress on the personal and even spiritual areas. To course correct would require additional time spent on the financial category, which, since we have a finite number of hours per day, week, and month, subtracts from the time spent on other areas. Luckily, my financial acumen was a high priority and the course correction was a pressing focus. The credit cards were paid off, with only two kept open and active, and I carry little to no credit card debt to this day. Ironically, my first job as a financial advisor was managing the portfolio assets of small business clients, likely fueled by my own firsthand "disruptive" learnings. However, regarding the associations, clearly, there is a totality connection across the dimensions. Each can be viewed as a separate facet, but directly influences and impacts the other areas with every discrete pivot. An important concept of The Diamond Advantage is that tensions in one area will influence facets in other areas as each inclusion will not sparkle alone, but luster will glisten, impacting the sheen of other facets within. Therefore, to optimize overall individual brilliance, an integrated strategy for next level success should include an authentic and full view of all that you are. Great news: no masks and no false pretenses required.

This customized solution will require reflection, and realization, prior to achieving the reward. The outcome of the reward is an integrated plan that details your roadmap to promote yourself without losing yourself or the ones you love. This powerful journey will likely be an awakening grounded in your core values and strengths. As the owner of your success, you are the author of the plan and can modify it as your personal goals shift and evolve with new inputs over time. This framework

I've coined as The Diamond Advantage is an analogy to explain the concepts of the process. The following chapters will discuss each of the five dimensions within the PRISM framework of The Diamond Advantage with thoughtful insight to guide the process.

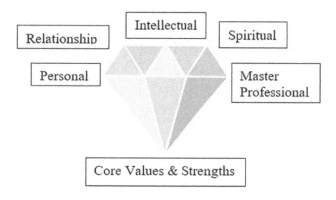

As a visual overview, think of the diamond shape or square with points north, south, east, and west for simplicity. Actually draw the shape on paper. Imagine that the bottom facet is labeled "core values and beliefs." Core values and beliefs are the foundation of who we are, and based on beliefs, our actions follow. First, through reflection, we will consider your individual core values and beliefs. Referring back to the diamond shape, the far left facet is labeled "Personal" and the far right is labeled "Master Professional." Although positioned on opposite sides of our gem prism, the connections within the construct impact and influence each other. The

Intellectual dimension assumes the top peak, on the left of the center, the Relationship position nestles between Personal and Intellectual, and on the right, the Spiritual locus is between Intellectual and Master Professional. At the center of it all is you, your core values and your unique strengths. The realization to enhanced brilliance is made through sequential progression of the PRISM framework as inspirational strategies are developed in support of the reward, your next level success. Before we begin this important work, let's get grounded in your why.

Your Why

Your why, or motivation to succeed, should get you energized and excited about pursuing your goals. Humble beginnings, in my opinion, served as a great motivator, not as an excuse to hide behind. It was the fuel that propelled me forward and still contributes to my drive today. As a young girl, I can recall the first time I saw a person of influence that looked like me on television. In was in the late 1980s on the prime time show *Dynasty,* a character named Dominique Deveraux. The character was played by Diahann Carroll, who went on to play other roles that I admire, but none left an impression like Dominique Deveraux. I don't quite remember the storyline, but I remember her, and her influence. She was a boss and exuded confidence. She called the shots, spoke articulately, and dressed impeccably. She was intelligent and knew her way around a deal. She had the respect of her colleagues as well as those who didn't care for her. She was a powerhouse in meetings and for me, symbolized the epitome of success. She inspired me and I wanted to be just like her. Probably a lot more subconsciously than consciously at first, there was a definitive shift that occurred that I still hold onto today and get excited about. I certainly didn't know how I was going to get there, but knew where I was headed. Dominique Deveraux became my why. Because of her influence, I was able to envision being like her. She helped to crystalize my vision with clarity, and the purpose followed in a meandering way. I credit that character for inciting what could be in me.

The imagining and reimaging is essential to drive success momentum. What's your why? Think about what drove your motivation long ago. Tap into those feelings and relive. Was it a promise to a loved one or a responsibility bestowed upon you? Was it a desire ignited by a particular experience or lack of an experience? Get grounded in your why and utilize it to help visualize your success. The below questions will help foster your success vision:

What does your success look like? Who is around and shares in your success? What skills are you using? Who benefits from your efforts? How do you spend most of your time? What impact are you making? Are you satisfied with your output?

What, if anything, would you do differently? What, if any, new skill sets are needed for your success? Write or journal your thoughts for your current success vision – we will revisit them later on in our journey.

Then, separately, if money was no object, what would you do for a living? How would you spend most of your time? What do you enjoy doing so much that you often don't realize how time passes when you're engaged in it?

How do the two answers compare? If there is a vast discrepancy, how can we get the response to the first set of questions closer and in more alignment to the second? Is alignment even possible? If not, can this enjoyed activity be increased in other areas of your life?

Your success vision is essential for motivation, commitment, and most importantly, for accountability. As you make progress through The Diamond Advantage framework, your success vision will likely become increasingly clear and lucid. For now, delight in reinvigorating your why as you begin your journey to promoting yourself to next level success. Take note of the details of your current success vision and add actual visual images where possible. As your future state becomes more defined, add additional detail to your vision. Be creative. Feel free to remove targets that are no longer relevant. Include all aspects that you consider part of your success, such as family, friends, and even your close network or tribe that advocate and support your advancement. Congratulations on completing your success vision.

Be present, engaged, and grateful for where you are today. Gratitude deals with being present and looks to the past, where ambition and unfortunately fear, are forward looking. Your success vison keeps you grounded to the past and energized in your voice for the future. It's an antidote to the inevitable fear that will creep into our intellect as a derailer. Commit to the decision that you will affirm your voice by taking action and revisiting your success vision daily. This is your starting point and we will build from there.

She believed she could~
So, she did.
– C.S. LEWIS

Media Trends – Women Having It All

Much of the focus to this point has been on the individual; however, shifting to broader views gives context to the climate to be navigated. There is certainly still a notion that women cannot have it all, considering the pulse on gender relations pertaining to a successful career and family.[4]

This notion that women can't have it all is not due to a lack of ambition, but rather a disconnect between social and business policy. For instance, in the case of the responsibilities of child rearing and caring for elderly parents, which more often fall upon women, flex scheduling and stair stepping careers are options that better allow meeting family obligations. These solutions, when integrated into your workplace, reduce the specific stressors of female professionals that impact performance. Comparably, industry thought leader Sheryl Sandberg, Facebook COO, who has a greater extensive support system than most, recognized the importance that women lean in and not disengage before they physically leave.[5]

Likewise, Sallie Krawcheck, former senior executive of Smith Barney and current LinkedIn Influencer with over 1.6 million followers, touts improvements needed in this space, including sponsorship, manager education and accountability, measurements of success, and flex arrangement without shame.[6]

A common theme I've observed for women to excel at parity with male counterparts is that good intent is characteristically at the core but goes awry in the midst of implementation. Have you noticed the same?

A clear example of a shift in mindset is observed in the YouTube video entitled "Like a Girl."[7]

This recording was viewed by nearly 63 million viewers at the time of this writing and prompts discourse fixed on the societal deviation of what it means for adolescents to be "like a girl" before the teenage years, and then shifts significantly to its derogatory or inferior connotation for middle-school age boys and girls alike. Without a self-checking mechanism, these parables can play into workplace dynamics. The tip to minimizing these negative thoughts is to recognize that they exist and counter them with positive mindsets. Simply pausing and affirming the positive serves as the "breaking mechanism." With practice, this regulation becomes more natural but will still resurface now and again without notice. Clearly, the paradox of gender diversity is complex and multifaceted. To some degree, customized solutions need to align with organizational culture, and primarily are unfinished business as progress in this area continues to develop, not quite as fast as many would expect. We have a ways to go for a true mindset shift for women. I'm optimistic, particularly if each of us, men and women, collectively decide to make a difference.

The prevalent and resounding discourse was that although there is a lack of content offering definitive solutions, the issue of women confidently articulating their voice is widespread at both junior and more senior levels of leadership. Women of the White

House Obama Administration utilized an approach called amplification, which allowed for their female executives' voices to be heard.[8]

Essentially, the women would repeat a point made by a prior female, reinforcing messaging while simultaneously giving recognition to that particular perspective. This approach was markedly effective in shifting women from being "invisible to visible." As referenced in a Harvard Business Review article,[9] a CEO of a Fortune 500 organization graciously admitted to his unintended oversight of several women in a meeting who presented similar views. Their commentary was followed by a male who recited the same view, and it was only then that he thought favorably of the concept. He realized this misstep afterward when a colleague privately brought this nuance to his attention while reviewing a recording of the meeting. Because amplification served its purpose in mitigating the gender dynamic at the highest office levels, a similar approach would be effective when integrated into our success journeys. In my experience, amplification is contagious! Start with yourself, by lifting up another woman executive, and the favor more often than not will be returned. I challenge you to make this adjustment in your next meeting or engagement. You won't regret it!

Chapter 4:

Cut, Color, Clarity ...Confidence

How you do anything~
Is how you do everything.
– T. HARV. ELKER

Your unique brilliance begins in the personal domain of The Diamond Advantage. This multifaceted glow is as unique to the individual as the cut, color, clarity, and carat is to any given precious stone. The challenging and disruptive environments that were part of your accomplished experience provide insight for your next level success promotion. The personal domain includes core values and strengths that correlate and impact the other areas of your life. Exploring this domain will begin to uniquely uncover what matters the most at the core and provide the foundation for your distinctive affinities to confidently determine next level success. To be clear, perfection is not an aim for this progression. In fact, the more transparent and authentic your approach, the more genuine the results. This experience is for you, by you, and may even feel a bit vulnerable. You owe it to yourself to remove any mask or other false pretense as you progress through the PRISM framework.

Perfectly Imperfect

As mentioned previously, a diamond stone is developed in the earth's mantle, or outer layer, approximately one hundred miles deep and under extreme temperatures up to 2,000° Fahrenheit. I reference this again due to the significance this disruption has to produce the cherished gem, akin to our success to personal brilliance. While the precious stone transformation can take between one to three billion years, only the rarest gems emerge in perfect condition.[10] It has been estimated that only 600 "perfect" diamonds between one to two carats (as defined by clarity grade) have existed.[11] Most often they are imperfect and contain varying amounts of internal inclusions and surface blemishes. In fact, a low clarity diamond magnified by ten will look identical to one with no inclusions at all.[12] Taking hints from nature, if these one-of-a-kind flawed precious stones have the ability to awe through the ages, based on universal demand, isn't the timeless beauty and appeal really embedded in the uniqueness that each stone illuminates? Likewise, your cut, color, clarity, and carat that make up your preferences, values, and strengths are in unique combination to you. Relish in confidence that each desirable characteristic is exactly as it should be.

Differentiated Brilliance: An Imperative from a Business Perspective

Malcolm Forbes defined diversity, or independent luminosity, as "the art of thinking independently together." On the surface, this may appear to be a simple concept, yet researchers have validated that for the number of cases where diverse teams achieve success, there is nearly an equivalent number representing failure.[13] A number of organizations are positioned as exemplars in this multicultural collaboration space, such as IBM, which has integrated diversity as a part of their organizational strategy.[14] Others, like Clorox, have touted that diversity drives innovation.[15] This seeming paradox of thinking independently, but together, has surfaced as a multifaceted challenge that begins at the team level and perpetuates at the organizational level.

The business imperative lies in the notion that in less than one generation, the demographic composition of the majority is forecasted to shift to diminishing percentages,[16] creating the opportunity for expanded diversity of thought and ultimately increasing value creation. Diverse teams under optimal conditions outperform homogenous teams consisting of excellent talent.[17] According to a McKinsey 2015 study,[18] material diversity benefits were realized at the organizational bottom line with 35% of ethnically diverse organizations outperforming their non-diverse counterparts. In addition, 15% of diverse gender organizations outperformed gender-partial counterparts. What do these stats mean for your success? Organizations need diversity of thought to thrive. This provides an indication that fully permits each of us to get comfortable with our unique gifts. The organizations that have women represented at the board level, for example, outperform those that do not. Friend, your unique value proposition is the key to your next level success.

For organizations to successfully compete in a global society, diversity of thought and expertise is essential to sustain innovation and creative solution-making to strategically differentiate them from rivals.[19]

Microsoft provided a view that to sustain innovation within organizations requires a diverse cultural orientation. The concept affirms the research at diverse team collaboration at the team or micro-level has real implications at the organizational, or macro-levels.

According to Microsoft,[20] these results exemplify that diverse collaboration – which is inclusive of disparate ideas, perspectives, and cultures – yields enhanced or disruptive innovation and thus should be considered an organizational asset. The critical notion illuminated by the above figure is that over time, a paradigm shift in diverse teams results in productivity and innovation sustained for the long-term. Instances where such a shift does not occur or is stagnated, the result likely has unfavorable impacts to the productivity and innovation change when compared to effects before the phenomenon occurred. The smaller change, observed preceding the team paradigm shift, is typically insufficient in sustaining an organization to compete in a global marketplace successfully.

Brilliance from a Position of Strength

When thinking about up-leveling, it may seem daunting as to the optimal place to start. So, let's start at the very beginning in the personal domain – your core values. Core values are described as your fundamental beliefs or guiding principles that influence behavior. Your values have much to do with how you were raised or traditional beliefs passed to you, lived personal and professional experiences, and cultural norms. Collectively, these inputs shape one's unique perspective in how they view the world and interpret occurrences.

In other words, an identical experience can impact behavior in different ways. Because of this phenomenon, becoming familiar and increasing awareness, or emotional intelligence, of the effect indicators have on behavior will facilitate improved reactive navigation, ultimately enhancing outcomes. Gathering perspective on core values is often effortless, particularly in the earlier years and as knowledge and experience is gained and becomes more refined. For example, earlier in careers compensation may have had a higher value, but later, work-life integration may assume greater precedence. Because our core values are the epicenter of our guiding thoughts, decisions, and judgment, when there is alignment with inherent core values, there is greater fulfillment, sense of being, and purpose. Taking a step to review intrinsic core values will establish the highest-priority virtues that characteristically mold our paths to unprecedented brilliance. The aim is to honor our value system and align with passion and strengths, creating a harmony or flow that opens space for radiance to not only shine but to beam with vivacity through a multiplier effect when in personal integrity.

The following exercise[21] will help identify your individual core values. Please take note of the suggested duration for each step. The timeframes encourage instinctive reactions rather than overthinking responses.

Step 1 – Take three minutes to review the list and check any value that resonates with your fundamental beliefs. Feel free to add any core value that may not be listed.

Core Values List

Abundance	Cleverness	Excellence	Inspiration
Acceptance	Community	Expressiveness	Intelligence
Accountability	Commitment	Fairness	Intuition
Achievement	Compassion	Family	Joy
Adventure	Cooperation	Friendships	Kindness
Advocacy	Collaboration	Flexibility	Knowledge
Ambition	Consistency	Freedom	Leadership
Appreciation	Contribution	Fun	Learning
Attractiveness	Creativity	Generosity	Love
Autonomy	Credibility	Grace	Loyalty
Balance	Curiosity	Growth	Making a Difference
Being the Best	Daring	Happiness	
Benevolence	Decisiveness	Health	Mindfulness
Boldness	Dedication	Honesty	Motivation
Brilliance	Dependability	Humility	Optimism
Calmness	Diversity	Humor	Open-Mindedness
Caring	Empathy	Inclusiveness	
Challenge	Encouragement	Independence	Originality
Charity	Enthusiasm	Individuality	Passion
Cheerfulness	Ethics	Innovation	Performance

Personal Development

Proactive

Professionalism

Quality

Recognition

Risk Taking

Safety

Service

Spirituality

Peace

Perfection

Playfulness

Popularity

Power

Preparedness

Punctuality

Relationships

Reliability

Resilience

Resourcefulness

Responsibility

Responsiveness

Security

Self-Control

Selflessness

Simplicity

Stability

Success

Teamwork

Thankfulness

Thoughtfulness

Traditionalism

Trustworthiness

Understanding

Uniqueness

Usefulness

Versatility

Vision

Warmth

Wealth

Well-Being

Wisdom

Zeal

Step 2 – Take two to three minutes to review the attributes identified in the prior step and list similar core values into groups with a comparable association. An example is provided below. This will create columns of similar attributes to identify trends.

Abundance

Growth

Wealth

Security

Freedom

Independence

Flexibility

Peace

Acceptance

Compassion

Inclusiveness

Intuition

Kindness

Love

Making a Difference

Open-Mindedness

Trustworthiness

Appreciation

Encouragement

Thankfulness

Thoughtfulness

Mindfulness

Balance

Health

Personal Development

Spirituality

Well-being

Step 3 – Finally, take two minutes to select one core value from the related list as the attribute with the highest value or meaning to you. An example is illustrated below.

Abundance	Acceptance	Appreciation	Balance
Growth	Compassion	Encouragement	Health
Wealth	Inclusiveness	Thankfulness	Personal Development
Security	Intuition	Thoughtfulness	
Freedom	Kindness	**Mindfulness**	Spirituality
Independence	Love		**Well-being**
Flexibility	**Making a Difference**		
Peace	Open-Mindedness		
	Trustworthiness		

Well done! You now have your Brilliance Baseline established. Reflect for a moment on your Brilliance Baseline and think about how you're honoring your core values in your personal and/or professional life. Rank each of the values established in order of importance. We'll reference these again in the future.

Everyone <has their own> genius~
But, if you judge a fish by its ability to climb a tree~
It will spend its whole life believing it is <foolish>.
— ALBERT EINSTEIN

Shift in Brilliance to Genius Zone

If you're like most, a relatively large portion of your time is spent on improving weaknesses. We live in a society where perfection, or perceived perfection, is the norm. The prevalence of air brushed pics, nips and tucks, and fantasy social media lives has placed undue pressure on society at large. Imbalanced performance appraisals and leaders who focus predominantly on areas of development are 22% more likely to have an actively disengaged employee.[22] Perpetuating a weakness-improvement campaign places limitations on accentuating individual brilliance and the magnitude and effectiveness of a personal value proposition. I implore you to shift your brilliance. By no means should shortcomings be ignored; however, shifting your brilliance to be more focused on strengths will dramatically expand the quality of output while increasing contentment in work. Joy!

I'm reminded of Renee, an ambitious achiever who excelled at her accounting role but was not stimulated beyond creating reports and dashboards. She certainly was better than good at it but the effort required of her to complete her given responsibilities was daunting. In fact, she cringed at the thought of each quarterly cycle, especially since it coincided with her physically getting either a terrible cold or sometimes even strep throat. This was clearly not a coincidence. As my mentee, I recommended she honor her Brilliance Baseline while still using her given strengths. After spending time to reassess her core values, she realized that she wasn't being challenged and that she preferred to be more creative and relationship-oriented in her daily work. It was vital that she be inclusive to her natural aptitude for quantitative metrics. Together we made a strategic plan of action and a year later Renee was in a strategy role that utilized her innate talents but also incorporated her desire for a big picture view and collaboration. She loves what she does and truly has found new energy for her work. Also, she's happy to report that the chronic colds and coughs have ceased. A shift in brilliance brought Renee closer to operating in her genius zone and she is well positioned for future success.

According to Google, talents are described as "a natural aptitude or skill" and are attributed to the innate way you think, feel, and behave. Typically the learning curve is not as steep for inherent talents as other attributes. Prince had a talent for music, Michael Jackson for performance, and Steve Jobs for innovation – even Serena Williams, who is still winning Grand slams in tennis immediately after giving birth to her baby. They each had a natural ability for a specific genre and their inborn talent, and although they were exemplary and nearly effortless when compared to others, they still placed a tremendous amount of focus on their genius (maniacal in most cases) and worked their craft beyond conceivable measures. Michael Jackson often recounted that he felt his entire childhood was lost due to the way emphasis developing his talent was positioned in his life. It is indeed talent that differentiates; operating within the genius zone brings a flow that allows energy, creativity, and intuition to magnify. Skill and knowledge are companions to talent, which allow talent to be organically fueled for further growth.

A Case for Multi-dimensional Leader Engagement

Organizations realize the importance of talent development. Talent strategies are essential for a thriving organization at the macro level, as well as individual growth at the micro level. Organizational behavior has evolved from a vertical one-directional approach to a state that exhibits shared vision between leader and follower.[23] This improved dynamic has resulted in augmented performance results, since employees that are engaged assume an ownership mentality that moves behavior beyond complacency and merely being compliant. This is the optimal space where leaders gain *discretionary effort* from their direct reports, which is essential to propelling an organization forward; these essential attributes can be incited by the leader.[24] Both positive and negative behavior is contagious in an organizational system, as elements are constantly influencing aspects within the culture.[25] There is a place for healthy speculation; however, negative or misaligned perspectives can potentially shift organizational dynamics to an undesired status.

Smith and Lewis[26] posited that binary decision making produces suboptimal results. As organizations compete in a global dynamic marketplace, what appear to be polarizing tenets should be considered comprehensively holding varying tensions concurrently; for example, learning and belonging, in which tension resides in being progressive versus adaptive to the norm; or belonging and organizing, which conflicts the need for individualization and conformance with the collective.[27] Organizations that produce multifaceted solutions.[28] that consider both inter- and intra-organizational objectives in dynamic environments will capture the lion's share of the success equation.[29]

Genius Zone at the Individual Level

Now that we've discussed the importance of talent strategies at the organizational level, let's pivot to the individual. The individual, or micro level, impacts the organization at the macro level in aggregate. It's important to understand how your individual influence impacts at the organizational level. The success paradigm is often linked to the value proposition you bring to the workplace. Omitting this connection is a misstep in conceptualizing how you specifically impact the collective. The areas of strength can be segmented into four domains: Relationship Builder, Influencer, Strategic Thinker, and Executer, or "RISE." The below exercise, Radiant RISE, will help you to determine your unique strategic differentiators or areas of strength. There are variations of this method currently used; however, Radiant RISE was specifically created as a component of The Diamond Advantage.

Step 1 – Take three minutes to review the attributes that make up each domain and select five attributes that you believe align with your inherent talents.

Relationship Builder	Influencer	Strategic Thinker	Executer
• Adapt	• Activate	• Analyze	• Achieve
• Connect	• Command	• Context	• Arrange
• Develop	• Communicate	• Forward Thinking	• Belief
• Empathic	• Compete	• Ideation	• Consistent
• Harmony	• Maximize	• Input	• Deliberate
• Inclusive	• Self-Assure	• Intellectual	• Discipline
• Individualization	• Significance	• Learner	• Focus
• Positive	• Winning Over	• Strategic	• Responsible
• Relate			• Restorative

Bear in mind, there is no right or wrong answer and it is likely that you have strengths in more than five characteristics. Choose your top five that you naturally and effortlessly align with. As validation, ask a trusted friend what attributes of strength come to mind when he or she thinks of you. Compare this to your selections and make a final judgment call on your five Radiant RISE Strengths. Below I share my Radiant RISE Strengths as an example.

Relationship Builder	Influencer	Strategic Thinker	Executer
• Adapt	• Activate	• Analyze	• **Achieve**
• Connect	• Command	• Context	• Arrange
• Develop	• **Communi-cate**	• Forward Thinking	• Belief
• Empathic	• Compete	• **Ideation**	• Consistent
• Harmony	• Maximize	• Input	• Deliberate
• Inclusive	• Self-Assure	• Intellectual	• Discipline
• **Individual-ization**	• Significance	• Learner	• Focus
• **Positive**	• Winning Over	• Strategic	• Responsible
• Relate			• Restorative

As a next step, take a moment to reflect on your responses. How are you leveraging your strengths? According to 2017 Strengths Development research,[30] in a survey of more than 10 million people globally, approximately one-third reported that they strongly agreed that they "have the opportunity to do what I do best every day." In terms of employee engagement and the linkages to productivity in employment, this insight positions a bleak narrative for individual engagement, and thus organizational longevity. The same report cited that associates who do have the opportunity to focus on their strengths are six times as likely to be engaged.

As a final step, take three minutes to determine what the potential advantages and disadvantages are of each of your Radiant RISE Strengths. For example, being positive is a beneficial attribute overall, but being unrealistically positive can pose a detriment to developmental opportunity. For me, I've learned that my natural affinity is to be a direct communicator, however in times of stress, for example meeting a compressed deadline, the strength becomes a potential negative due to overuse of the direct communication. Having this awareness and a trusted peer that can privately point out instances where there may have been opportunity for improvement helps me close this gap. With practice, I've learned to overcome and strengthen this attribute greatly.

Now that the Brilliant Baseline and Radiant RISE are established, we should revel in confidence that the exploration in the personal domain has provided insight on our uniquely designed cut, color, and clarity blueprint. Being more you brings a flow of positive energy, creating space for your genius zone to luminate excellently.

Your Confident Voice

Emotional intelligence often glistens in a narrow ridge where you hold your perspective, yet strive for openness for others to collaborate and provide input. Social scientists often look to nature and the physical sciences to glean insight centered on intrinsic behavior, interactions, and relationships. Analyzing a leadership approach in the absence of emotional or cultural context would omit the connections with a leader's approach. From an individual or leader perspective, Moore and Mamiseishvili[31] stated that a leader's emotional intelligence should be inclusive to the leadership paradigm, as the leader's beliefs, values, and motives stem from one's emotional intelligence. Wheatley, with a slightly different slant, put forth a view of significant correlation of universal systems' integral elements.[32] The concept supported the ideal of a disorderly system having an influence on the comprehensive make-up of the system in its entirety. This research suggested that seemingly-unconnected entities are fundamental ingredients to the overall system.[33] What was once thought of as irregularity or disorder in science systems can be perceived as purposeful stability; the paradox of chaos and uniformity then brings a comprehensive structure to the system with unique nuances that feed newness to the thriving system.

According to Wheatley, neither disorder nor stability is superior to the other, as both attributes are necessary in system processes to obtain continual growth within the system – for the leader, for the subordinate, and for the team. [34] This system-based thinking, therefore, suggests that within any given system – for example, within an organization – individual elements interconnecting is perceived as just random links, but also as integrating influences and non-visible energy fields that interrelate.[35] What appears to be polarizing, and perhaps an outlier on the surface, leads to a complementary disorder or balancing correspondences, which incites distinctiveness within the organizational system. These distinctive gradients introduce novel characteristics that serve as an input to progressive growth evolutions.

If a working team is beheld as such a system within a larger organizational system, what then occurs scientifically as individuals convene? Seagal and Horne[36] provided a means for understanding collective capability by linking social research to the science of the human system. An individual's unique affinities inform discrete learnings and assumptions of environmental and individual experiences through distinctive filters.[37] Because each inimitable expression or interpretation, although congruent, comprehensively acts as complements with no one type superior to the other,[38] it can be reconciled that a team should consist of a variety of dimensions creating healthy tensions for augmenting performance. As one simultaneously balances the narrow ridge[39] of disparate perspectives to maintain one's own perspective while being open to others, one physiologically taps into an emotional space of uncertainty.

What does this all mean for you who is trying to get to your next level success? Random actions will not drive your power forward. Action, even incrementally, should be purpose driven. The Diamond Advantage framework addresses actionable and purposeful implementation through developing a customized plan – the output of this framework. Knowing your Diamond Blueprint is the first step to creating your success plan, the second, is taking action. The narrow ridge of holding your own perspective while being open to others flickers with an uncertain glow, however it's vital to be true to self with a mindset that permits room for new and novel ideals to extend current thinking.

Your Personal Polish

As mentioned, the relational matrix within the PRISM domains – Personal, Relationships, Intellectual, and Master Professional – are indeed connected in affiliation with one another. Extraordinary gains and deficiency limitations in each of the discrete domains alike will influence the entire system. With this in mind, personal and self-care is an imperative. Our personal prowess, or SERGES, as I like to call it, includes Sleep, Energy, Rejuvenation, Gastronomy, Exercise, and Stress Management. If I may, I'd like to add Style. Yes, style; making SERGESS our acronym for your personal keys essential for success. Although most of us are sheroes in our own right, deficiency in any one of these personal polish facets can create imbalances that will challenge our abilities to thrive.

- Sleep. Adequate sleep is the way we physically recharge. If this is out of proportion, course correct quickly. Sleep routines should include unplugging devices, quiet time with yourself, and perhaps chamomile tea or a glass of red wine. A morning routine often starts from the night before. A good night's rest leads to a refreshed morning with new ideas and perspectives that were "downloaded" during cozy slumbers. Do what works best for you to get several REM cycles in per night. Airplane mode is a remarkable device feature. Let's choose when to engage in the digital stratosphere.

- Energy. Energy management typically has a direct correlation to our productivity. Energy goes where our attention goes; therefore, spend calories on the highest-priority items earlier in the day. Time block daily tasks to ensure your energy is managed accordingly. For example, schedule when you will check emails, make phone calls, and, most importantly, schedule white space time. If you are producing every moment of the day, no time will have been spent on strategy, innovation, and growth. Make it a routine to set several hours a week for forward-thinking activity. Time block wherever possible; my response to almost everything is, "Let me put that on my calendar." My calendar integrates personal and professional activities. With that said, one of the most valuable leadership lessons that I learned from my coach was to delegate the not critical/not urgent in addition to the critical/urgent items. In considering the grid below (adapted from Eisenhower's Urgent/Important Principle), take a moment to populate it with daily, weekly, monthly, quarterly, and annual routines.

	Urgent	Not Urgent
Critical		
Not Critical		

Of those routines, which are you able to delegate in order to focus your time on the highest-priority work and decisions? I've populated mine below with a few suggestions.

	Urgent	Not Urgent
Critical	• Deadlines • Taxes • Annual Physicals	• Mid-term deadlines • Planned activities • Relationship Building • Personal Development
Not Critical	• Meetings • Returning phone calls • Grocery shopping	• Surfing the internet • Vacation • Social Media updates

Now, I do recognize that some of the populated activities are up for debate; vacation, for instance, is categorized as not urgent/not critical, but truth be told, it often gets elevated to critical status depending on other stressors. The provided example is for illustrative purposes; be liberated to customize it as you see fit. The ultra-successful have mastered this concept. My mentor, as the exemplar, no longer grocery shops, does dry cleaning, or cleans house. He has a personal shopper, a social media brander, and I could go on. From his perspective, he would rather pay someone else to do not critical or not urgent tasks to save his energy to make the critical decisions. My mentor, J.T., has double digit businesses, is always in a dark suit, and manages his nine-digit portfolio with supreme efficiency from his iPhone. The opportunity cost of expending calories on less-prioritized duties negates the tremendous potential upside. Numerous sources, including WSJ, NYT, and Forbes, corroborate[40] that decision fatigue is taxing on our executive center due to the average of 35,000 decisions we make per day. Stiletto or wedges? Latte or cappuccino? Highway or freeway? Times New Roman or Arial? Paperclip or staple? Our everyday decisions can be endless. Even though we each are granted a time-boxed 86,400 seconds per day, 35,000 daily decisions seems unnerving as this reasonably calculates to a decision rendered every two and a half seconds. Uber successful individuals, including our presidential leaders, Mark Zuckerberg, and even Simon Cowell have deliberately reduced the number of mundane decisions they make per day by adopting a "uniform" of sorts. Managing energy undoubtedly is an imperative as we SERGESS in our personal prowess.

- ◆ Rejuvenation. Work hard, play hard, rejuvenate, and repeat. Whatever activity – or no activity, for that matter – allows you restoration and reinvigoration, embrace it and add it to your weekly routine. Spa, golf, reading, writing, or

Indy 500 racing (as in the case of Danica Patrick) – we each have our rejuvenation pastime of choice. Make sure you make time for you.

- Gastronomy. Our nutrition paradigm is to include green drinks, protein, plenty of water, and minimal carbs. You are already well versed in the proper palette. Let's sincerely take action on this. Wellness strategies are vital to our overall well-being. Congratulations in advance for up-leveling this important faction of your personal domain.

- Exercise. Yes, exercise. Wake up, workout. In my experience, getting into motion actually sustains daily mental dexterity, keeps us physically fit, and, most importantly, reduces stress. Get an accountability partner, wearable technology, and get your motion goals alive. Even incremental change will have residual benefits. Make it fun!

- Stress management. This one is critical because stress can significantly impede you well beyond the personal domain. High achievers under elevated and prolonged levels of stress are 46% more likely to be subject to an autoimmune disease.[41] With our incredible facets proverbially connected, disease is the way our bodies let us know that we're not at ease. We cannot afford to allow this area to go awry. It's too detrimental, the downside is impactful, and the stakes are too high.

♦ And finally, my favorite: style. Your style is part of your brand. You are a brand and upholding the essence of your brand is embedded in your presence (both in person and online), communication, attitude, emotional intelligence, and integrity, as well as physical appearance. Sallie Krawcheck once said, "I once read that the first part of your career is about dressing to be seen as successful, and then once you're successful, it's about dressing to be seen as accessible. Hence, my leather jackets! I love leather."[42] Also, Arianna Huffington shared, "I would love to see all women join the #stylerepeats movement! Instead of dealing with the stress of always feeling like you have to wear something new for every occasion which, let's face it, puts us at a huge competitive disadvantage with men, just wear something you love, again and again."[43] These trailblazing women are certainly on to something, insightfully freeing up mental space to leave capacity to dedicate our attention to what matters to us the most. A simple, but novel idea; if we all participate, the stigma (and financial commitment) for "one-time wears" diminishes.

Now that we have completed SERGESSing our personal prowess, let's reflect on where we stand with each. How satisfied are you with each of the facets in this domain? Take a moment to rate each of the personal SERGESS attributes from 1 to 5. At this point, I'm twinkling with enthusiasm that the personal domain exploration is complete. Revel in your excitement and glow with confidence. Your radiance warmly radiates over the horizon.

Pretty women wonder where my secret lies.
I'm not cute or built to suit a fashion model's size
But when I start to tell them,
They think I'm telling lies.
I say,
It's in the reach of my arms,
The span of my hips,
The stride of my step,
The curl of my lips.
I'm a woman
Phenomenally.
Phenomenal woman.

– DR. MAYA ANGELOU

Chapter 5:

Intentional Relational

You make me laugh,
even when I'm not in the mood to smile.
— ANONYMOUS

"You make me laugh, even when I'm not in the mood to smile" is the priceless and intangible sentiment that we value from our cherished relationships. As the highest order species that walks the planet, humans are differentiated through a complex intellect as well as our need for a sense of belonging and, in the purest essence, to be loved. I think about Dylani, who from all accounts would appear to have it all: a husband that made a great income as a real estate investor, the grand 6,000 square foot house, vacations in Milan, and all the other bells and whistles that went along with the lifestyle. She and I were friends for many years from our days living in New York. I was so proud of her because she was the epitome of success and made it out of the hard knocks. We sat on her back porch drinking Blueberry Slim Life tea on one picturesque spring afternoon. I gazed out, just taking in her well-manicured lawn, the larger-than-life peonies that ranged from the most vibrant pink to the softest baby hue of barely there pink. Pink and peonies are two of my favorite things. Wow, the wonderful life. I turned to my dear friend and complimented her on her meticulous home; each of the five bedrooms boasted 5-star suite status, each with an adjoining private bathroom and sitting area with a fireplace. Her response was a bit uncanny. She looked down, fiddling with her recently-upgraded wedding ring. "Yeah," she said, "It's a large house but it has no love. It's just empty." I was mortified; however, while I showed no outward sign of my shock, somehow in the depth of my intuition I was not surprised. I held her hand reassuringly and said, "Whatever you need, I'm here for you." We sat silently for a while, no words needed to be spoken. She knew that I would be there whatever the need, both large and small, even if it meant sitting with her in silence. Some time had passed, I squeezed her hand and said, "Hey, no need to be a duck right now, it's me!" She looked up, smiled, and let out a hearty laugh. We hugged and her energy shifted. We both knew that it may not be easy but together we'll get through. I made her laugh even when she wasn't in the mood to smile – that's what your tribe is for. Cherished relationships are there to encourage, to support, and to bring out the best in you. I'm happy to have been called friend.

"The duck" was our secret code for the mask that we often have to wear in trying moments for survival and protection, to appear just as graceful, poised, and unrattled in intense situations. The duck is a protection mechanism that appears graceful on the surface but full of high energy that nearly swirls out of control on the inside, similar to the rampant gestures underneath the water's surface as witnessed as our flying friends glide across the water. There's such beauty in having a tribe where there are no masks, no ducks, no pretenses, just you. This support system is integral to sustained success. Having it all means getting to the next level of defined success while preserving the relationships we care about the most.

The Relationship Gamut

Our discussion thus far predominantly centered on close personal relationships that matter. The relationship gamut, however, extends well beyond the circle of our inner tribe. The Diamond Relational Watermark below illustrates concentric relationship circles that place the individual at the core. As each relational sphere moves outward in tiers, it is representative of individuals who influence life transformations less directly.

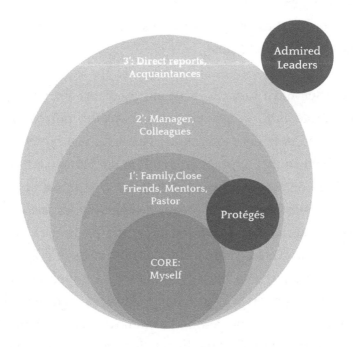

Tier 1 – The primary level or *"The Gut Checkers"* includes a tribe of family, close friends, mentors, and/ or religious leaders. These are the individuals who are comfortable in providing full transparent feedback. The value at this level is authentic grounding and confidence in the truth. This level believes in your abilities wholeheartedly, even when you doubt yourself, providing a strong motivational force to continue to press on, often learning lessons from their own experiences. We've observed time and again fallen stars that no longer had Gut Checkers in their lives make fatal missteps that carried a mortal cost. This primary level should be viewed as your personal board of directors. This group should be diverse in expertise, gender, and culture to optimize the collective sage advice and coaching.

Tier 2 – At the secondary level, or *"The Skeptics,"* are managers and colleagues who play a more cynical role in attributing developmental evaluation through 360° feedback. This appointed group provides candid views through formal performance appraisals incorporating both technical and soft-skill competence. Ironically, their skepticism characteristically fuels the drive to achieve. Be open to receive feedback and take action on this insight.

Tier 3 – Finally, at the tertiary level, or *"The Bench,"* are direct reports and acquaintances that are not as forthcoming and direct with commentary, but serve as a sense of community and belonging as well as the current industry standard, and provide an external perspective. Often times, with finesse, it's what's not said rather than what is in this group that is of significance.

Protégés and Admired Leaders – The individuals whom you mentor and admired leaders also influence the relational dynamic. A mentor relationship is bidirectional in that both the protégé and the mentor are benefitting. For example, my protégés have taught me how to be a better listener, a better coach, and have provided perspective on emerging distribution channels and trends. Admired leaders, who inspire from a distance through their actions and achievements, relationally influence our thinking through their lived example. Justice Sonia Sotomayor is my admired leader. She excelled to great achievements despite her humble beginning in Bronx, New York. Because of her exemplary accomplishments, she serves as my shero. Your admired leader does not necessarily have to have widespread notoriety; it may be the community leader that consistently volunteers with a servant's heart – unknown but impactful beyond measure.

Nonetheless, all tiers of The Diamond Relational Watermark are critical, as each serves a specific and needed purpose. Success strategies are informed by the incremental and disruptive transformations that create novel intervals for new and refined brilliance to radiate. Before we engage on a reflective exercise regarding your own Diamond Relational Watermark, I want to bring awareness to another group that didn't make the watermark; I call them *"The Haters."* This acknowledgement is made without empowering this clique, but they are important to bring into the fold – they serve a purpose too. Firstly, recognize that The Haters' issues are not with you, but with themselves. They ought to be kept at a distance but often provide clues as to what you're doing *right*. Their criticism should be taken with a grain of salt, but I stay curious to the Hater perspective. If nothing else, it's a data point that provides a comprehensive perspective. The Haters let you know when you're in the right lane. Collectively, this dynamic relational construct, with fleeting cut, color, and clarity, randomly influencing the overall system, not only provides a foundation for a hyper-augmented support system, it also provides a realm for co-creation through the influencing process. The input from the various layers in the Diamond Relational Watermark creates sparks of stimulus that add to the overall luminescent system. Over time, this paradigm can incite mere glimmers into brawny flames due to the transfer of tacit knowledge, information that is learned, informal, and difficult to codify. The critical exchange of tacit knowledge can be equated to Grandma's cake recipe that only she knows how to perfect with "a little of this and a little of that." From a business perspective, it's the unwritten rules, the landmines that we can't afford to touch. For many of us who are first-generation college educated, this is a very vulnerable area and costly to learn only through firsthand experiences. Building a solid network can be the differential between meeting versus exceeding performance expectations. A solid network is essential to thrive both in corporate and entrepreneurial settings. Your network is often indicative of your net worth.

Now that we assessed each area of the Diamond Relational Watermark, let's delve into who your primary level Gut Checkers, secondary level Skeptics, tertiary level Bench, and Protégés and Admired Leaders are, and also recognize Haters. Take a moment to identify each level within your personal watermark. List the names of individuals, starting with the Gut Checkers, followed by the secondary Skeptics, your Bench, and so forth. Complete each area of the watermark. What relational changes would you want to make, if any? Should you reposition or add anyone to the watermark? What relationships should you further develop?

Dylani's Outcome

Remember my friend Dylani, who was in a miserable relationship with her significant other? Her situation did get worse before it got better. Improvements didn't occur until they created an alliance and true partnership to work on the negative dynamic. I can say that the relationship did recover, with coaching, guidance, and being intentional. The improvement in this meaningful relationship, due to the connectivity and flow to other domains in her personal PRISM, opened opportunities that became very rewarding and fulfilling. She began doing consulting work from her home-based office, and quickly moved up the ranks at her firm. According to Dylani, she would not change her experience, because the journey would not have brought her to where she is today; happy, at peace, doing work she loves, and most importantly, joy-filled.

> *The most desired gift*
> *Is not diamonds, chocolate, or roses.*
> *It is focused attention.*
> **– Hplyrikz.com**

> *Energy goes where attention flows.*

Coach, Mentor, and Sponsor to Sparkle

I often refer to coaches, mentors, and sponsors as the bridge to work-life integration. In addition to delegation as mentioned previously, another method that speeds implementation is hiring the experts! But first, let's determine the difference between each and the role they might assume in furthering development. A coach guides and instructs, typically to refine a skill set learn a new one. This individual can be a manager or someone referred by your manager. If the coach is within your organization, assume this person has a direct line of communication to whomever referred him or her and will provide updates accordingly. A mentor relationship has a distinct difference because the mentorship is a trusted advisory dynamic. There is a code of conduct in this relationship where confidentiality should be held to the uppermost standard. This is a good place to discuss how to navigate other challenging situations. And finally, your sponsor is one who advocates on your behalf, frequently without your knowledge, as in the opening case study of this book. Attracting a sponsor is based not only on performance, but on your brand equity and potential for future elevation within your organization. Many organizations have formal mentorship programs, but sponsorship, on the other hand, is organic because the sponsor utilizes professional influence on your behalf. In an ideal scenario, a coach, mentor, and sponsor are needed for you to truly sparkle and differentiate yourself from peers. In fact, a number of mentors in varying genres and expertise are optimal to tap into a customized board of mentors well-suited for you to gain insight exponentially. Who is in your board of mentors currently? What areas in your board are lacking? Who can help you obtain that area of limited expertise?

Better than a thousand days of diligent study~
Is one day with a great teacher.
— **JAPANESE PROVERB**

A Pivot to the Organizational Case

As organizations adopt greater efficiency practices, such as trending toward a matrixed environment, greater collaboration is required to achieve optimal effects – particularly as organizations move toward one global society. The key elements in the quest to sustain greater efficiencies call for organizational adaptability and a discrete shift in accountability as integral organizational attributes to successfully compete with rivals.[44]

As improved adeptness practices are adopted, greater relational connectivity is required to achieve optimal effects, particularly as society iterates toward one global community. As a result of globalization, there is a distinct effort to raise the bar of creative solutions through diverse perspectives at the individual, team, and organizational levels. This would require the attention of strategic leadership both at the micro and macro tiers of the organization[45] requiring both linear and collaborative leadership networks throughout the organizational system.[46]

Informal and formal structures affect the potential of networks of relationships within an organization and can potentially impact the organization's sustainability. Utilizing "Recasting the Role of CEO: Transferring the Responsibility for Change: How Leaders Can Tap the Creative Energy of Employees,"[47] Nayar categorized the concept that leadership can affect an organization's ability to adapt to the role network. The convergence between informal and formal organizational structure and the leader's ability to adapt informs the organization's environment, and ultimately influences performance. Through theoretical analysis, the significance of appropriate collaborative structures that align with business strategy and bolster a culture of shared knowledge[48] have emerged, providing perspective and insight garnered from this literature review.

Trust, Integral to the Relational Paradigm

In a recent study, Goodwin et al.[49] focused on the implication of trust in transformational leadership. These researchers analyzed the empirical evidence gathered from a case study of leader-follower pairs. The participants of the study completed a survey to garner perspectives on trust with their immediate manager. Based on the findings, trust plays a significant role in a transformational leadership dynamic. Researchers have identified that if trust positions as moderator, then the full potential of transformational leadership may not be realized; however, if trust is a mediator, then it may be considered an outcome of the relationship [50] Whether further study implications determine that trust be present at the onset of team establishment – a moderator – or that it be developed as the team progresses – a mediator

–it has been determined through historical evidence to be a core tenet to successful team execution.

The results of the Goodwin et al. study[51]provided a model to frame future study implications that seek to gain insight on how trust correlates to transformative relationships in diverse teams. In Lauring and Selmer's study,[52]these scholars affirmed the link between diverse teams and trust. The current study had the aim to build upon Goodwin et al.'s[53] study to determine further insight into the association effects, especially attuned to the culture, gender, and generational variances within a transformative team. This insight can be leveraged as it's applied to our lives. We now know that our differences, what make us unique, are our strengths. These differences, particularly when working in a team setting, ideally create a healthy tension, but when the awareness of self and the impact it potentially has on others is low, this creates mistrust. There's a fine line with compromising your best self to meld into a team. The goal is to be an individual; in your brilliance, you allow others to do the same.

Leadership Impacts Organizational Adaptability

Leadership is thought to exist at every level of an organization. Informal and formal networks both within and external to the organization are integral to the organizational strategy.[54] The organizational structure, therefore, is integral to the success of formal and informal feedback loops required for long-term success. Complex systems abound with boundaries that are defined through social constructs.[55] These non-linear systems interconnect through feedback loops and nested relationships.[56] Although intangible, theses boundaries are real and grounded in the organization's cultural fabric. Any given organization can benefit from strong channels that integrate shared knowledge across the organization. As organizations seek to collaborate across business units and functions, and even within a global footprint, timely and accurate communication can be a challenge. The use of technology can be used to leverage speed for execution through strong communication conduits.[57] Ultimately, an "us-them" mentality limits inclusivity; although relational boundaries are symbolic in nature, they can potentially have detrimental effects on the organization's long-term trajectory.[58]

Network Theory Impacts Organizational Adaptability

Multilevel network theory[59] centers on the notion that leadership penetrates all levels of an organization regardless of station, and does not exclusively reside at the upper tiers of the hierarchy. This dynamic system will increase the entrepreneurship and ownership perspectives collectively of the organization, thereby increasing the discretionary effort of the collective. Harnessing the potential of these nested networks[60] will have material and residual effects to long-term realized gains. According to Nayar,[61] transitions occur in the organization from a leader top-down approach to a self-contained and governed environment. This strategic approach of macro and micro view assessment[62] is not absent of inherent challenges. The challenge to this approach is that it may consume a great deal of time depending on the complexity of the situation and the collaborative nature that may require a number of group working sessions, particularly to penetrate and adapt this approach to the lower ranks of the organization. Nonetheless, this strategy will minimize emotional injection in the decision-making and organizational strategy process, ensuring rigor and a structured approach to comprehensive evaluation during decision making. As such, the organization transitions from a leader top-down approach to a self-contained and governed environment, introducing elements of non-vertical leadership. This shift provides new norms where an ownership mindset is employed. It is certain that relationships, both formal and informal, collectively have a material impact on an organization's ability to thrive.

In sum, relationship and network dynamics are essential both for organizations and for personal reasons. It's clear why the relationships in your life are so meaningful and what would be lost in their absence, which is in line with the core values that were uncovered. A solid network is critical to your success.

Chapter 6:

Intellectually Curious, A Childlike Wonder

Approach the world
with a childlike wonder~
Intellectually curious,
in magnificent amazement.
— DR. HEATHER SIMONE

Our discussion of The Diamond Advantage framework will now center on the intellectual domain of the PRISM. Intellectual curiosity is an ongoing spark that allows growth expansion to continually occur. This learning mindset is multi-dimensional in that it should go beyond your daily work. The ultra-successful have one habit in particular that is common amongst this elite group. The average CEO reads sixty books per year.[63] Digital, in particular, is transforming the speed change and disrupting the prior norms at unprecedented levels. The move from sluggish and loud dial-up internet access to the current state of digital that includes worldwide access in split seconds and global communication though social media has occurred in less than one generation. Compare it to the length of time taken for the adoption of color television, only one type of digital disruption, first introduced in the United States in the early 1950s and not widespread in most countries until the mid-to-late 1970s.[64] By modest estimate, disruption is occurring at least three times faster than it was in the prior generation.

Being a voracious learner is table stakes due to the unparalleled digital age. As you know, the Diamond strategies span across dimensions, as inflections in one area impact others. The intellectual domain is no different; therefore, taking a comparable comprehensive view, the learning in this area should not be limited to just professional on-the-job experiences. Exceeding expectations of your current role is not enough for disruptive growth. Only when we expand beyond our current and immediate knowledge base do we increase our value proposition. The goal is not to be a subject matter expert in everything, but to know your craft extraordinarily, and your other areas of interest enough to be dangerous. If we accept that professional and personal facets are indeed influencing each other, then pastimes will positively affect professional learnings. Because we're inundated with the information age competing for our attention, being deliberate about how we spend our time has become even more important. The wealthy, defined as those with an annual income over $150k, are said to read for self-improvement, education, and success while obsessing over biographies for inspiration. The population outside of that criterion focuses more time on reading and engaging in activity purely for entertainment.[65]

Disorderly Is in Order

Research supports significant correlation of universal systems' integral elements, although disorderly, having an influence on the comprehensive make-up of the system in its entirety. The data suggests that seemingly-unconnected entities are fundamentally ingredient to the overall system.[66] What was once thought of as irregularity or disorder in science systems can be perceived as purposeful stability; the paradox of chaos and uniformity then brings a comprehensive structure to the system with unique nuances that feed newness to the thriving system.

According to Wheatley,[67] neither disorder nor stability is superior to the other as both attributes are necessary in system processes to obtain continual growth within the system, for the leader, for the subordinate, and for the team Similar to the system thinking concepts, each areas in The Diamond Advantage framework is a discrete areas that stands alone, yet improvements and/ or declines in each domain impacts the overall system. What may appear to be an isolated input, is in fact, part of a comprehensive construct. The fine details not only complement the system, but create distinctiveness. These distinctive gradients introduce novel characteristics that serve as an input to progressive growth evolutions. A competitive edge is what emerges as a result of value innovation disruptive properties. The anticipated increase in the value curve from creation to the end product is achieved as a competitive edge byproduct as undiluted innovation seeks purely to innovate. This quality end product that developed through innovation is often rewarded with dominance over competitors[68] both for the individual and at the organizational level. For individuals creating a strategy for next level success, this tells us that your competitive edge is what makes the difference in distinguishing yourself in your area of expertise. Leaning into what makes you special, your gifts and talents, creates your unique competitive edge.

Pastimes Abound

Intellectual curiosity goes beyond industry conferences. Whether your avid pastime is creating art, diving, gardening, chess, understanding bitcoin, live musicals, or something else, there is something to be learned in it all. Leisure activities typically fall into the following categories: social activities, collecting, sports, enrichment, creative, and domestic. Leveraging the digital revolution through e-books, podcasts, sound bites, and social media is only one way to gain knowledge and refine skills. Color outside of the lines, my friend. For me, traveling satisfies an intellectual curiosity for a number of reasons that cannot be learned from any textbook. Immersing myself into another culture and learning about its people provides rich perspective. In traveling to South America, the Caribbean, United Arab Emirates, Europe, and South Africa with confidence, I've gained personal insight that we are more alike than we are different. Universally, the North Star is the same: provide the best for your family, obtain the finest possible education for your children, discover passion and purpose to live meaningfully, while honoring a Higher Source or God. Through discrete firsthand travel experiences, a veil has been removed from my eyes where deeper perspectives, only gained through travel connections in totality, have emerged. How do these learnings show up? They impact how I treat others both personally and professionally. It gives greater appreciation for my journey, and others' journeys and histories. Sure, I could have gotten to this revelation by other means, but for me this passion was a result of treks across the globe.

Before we engage in a reflective exercise, it's important to note the bi-modal benefits of the intellectual domain. For one, it satisfies a curiosity with enjoyment that aligns with individual core values and strengths. Secondly, it lends to a continuous learning paradigm that augments other areas of the comprehensive domains. As an added bonus, leisurely activity that incites joy will reduce stress and anxiety, boosting a lasting positive or benevolence effect when integrated into reoccurring routines.

Intellectually Curious Exercise – As a brief reflective exercise, take a few minutes to reflect on the following: What leisure activity stimulates you in an unexpected way? How does this add to your value proposition? Is there anything you want to do differently in this space?

Diamond Habit Mindset

Research has shown that on average it takes twenty-one days and up to two months to make a habit, and longer for more complex routines.[69] Numerous studies of the habits of highly effective people include having a productive morning routine, being purposeful about how you're spending your time, being an avid learner, and building solid networks – all great activities that will drive productive behavior. There is no question that those activities are very much a means to increase effectiveness. Let's take it a step further to discuss the mindset one should have before engaging in habit forming endeavors. There is a mindset or way of thinking that will facilitate other core tenets that aid in driving successful habits. Namely, confidence in taking initiative by taking calculated risks and understanding that failure is a part of growth. We hear time and again that the hardest part is getting started on a new venture that we're seeking to incorporate into our routines. The confidence to pursue that new initiative is action oriented. We sometimes overthink processes and become our own hindrance by obstructing needed action. Our concerns about being excellent and perfect impede the ability to take the first step. I embolden you to cast perfectionism aside and power forward, imperfectly. Don't let self-doubt rear its ugly head because you're intelligent enough to refine where needed once progression has begun. Don't be immobilized by analysis paralysis – or fear, for that matter. Progress does not have to be perfect. I promise there will be opportunity to adjust where needed. What would be disgraceful is a missed opportunity to optimize your brilliance. Join me in the movement to make progress, not perfection. Progress wins over perfection every single time.

The second part of the Diamond Habit mindset is the idea that failure is integral to the growth process. Sounds counterintuitive, but is it? Even with our innate gifts and talents, rigor is essential to enhance our craft. It has been said that ten thousand hours of practice is a requisite to attain mastery in any given genre.[70] Ten thousand hours is approximately 417 days – of practice. In those ten thousand hours to the genius zone, failure is inevitable and in fact, becomes the prodigal teacher. Expect to have missteps and recover from the learnings. A mental fortitude of commitment and dedication to hone a craft would need to be tied to personal why motivation to make a logical rationale for the necessary dedication of substantial amounts of resources. Again, reminding us of the need to view central development opportunities in the comprehensive, and not in isolation of one another. Take a stand to not let self-doubt impede your confidence in initiative or the realization that failure is fundamental to growth. Make the decision – what waits on the other side is very much worth it!

Amira's Jams

Amira, a pediatric nurse, has had a passion for all things wellness for as far back as she can remember. Her decision to go into the health field was no surprise to those who knew her. It satisfied her intellectual curiosity as well as her quest to help others. She became the go-to person at work and at home to remedy most common ailments. She knew about alkalinity, inflammation, and, more recently, how to decipher the gluten-free and organic labyrinth. Through her piqued interest, she began creating novel flavors of jams and jellies that had virtually no trace of added sugar or artificial ingredients. They were an instant hit and soon her Saturdays were filled with preparing the incoming orders with her two helpers, her daughter and son, in tow. Her children enjoyed "having a job" and she enjoyed spending time with them while doing something she treasured.

The word about Amira's jams spread quickly and she was soon shipping her delicacy to nearby states. She was wise and continued to reinvest in her hobby-turned-business. She had the idea one day to make salsa with the same concept of healthy appeal without sacrificing taste. She added black beans and other surprises to her salsa that kept her clients intrigued. She literally became the Chief of Secret Sauce. Amira is the first to admit that the business aspect of her jams was intimidating. Her original interests certainly led to other unexpected learnings that she benefitted from. She is now astute on financial budgeting, inventory forecasts, and leading a team, skill sets that will certainly be advantageous in her nursing role. Amira even has interns assisting with routine business duties to facilitate workflow. It's fulfilling her more than she ever imagined and she plans to continue to scale her business progressively. In her case, her initial intention was not to be an entrepreneur, but to simply delve into her piqued interests. Acting on that spark of interest has led to acquired skills that have benefitted other areas of her life. The best part? She's having fun through it all. What is your "secret sauce" and what is still on your to-do list? What's preventing you from percolating intellectual curiosity with a childlike wonder?

Sparkle Delights Thus Far

So, where are we in The Diamond Advantage PRISM framework? We have explored the personal, relationship, and intellectual domains and have covered plenty of ground. We recognize there is a customized solution to the success paradigm based on an overview of the five-dimensional Diamond Advantage framework that will bring clarity and significance to the decision of next level success while staying connected to our important relationships. We also acknowledge that it is necessary to get connected to unique core values and strengths, uncovering what matters most at the core through individual personal reflections in the first step in the personal domain of the framework. We then explored why the relationships are so meaningful and what would be lost without them. The focus was particularly on the needed support and mentorship that some relationships provide. In the absence of support, a void would exist in our lives. This journey so far is based on the core values that were uncovered. With just two domains remaining on our journey to success, clarity should begin to set into focus. The spiritual and master professional are the final areas of discovery. Relish in your progress. We've accomplished much and are past the mid-point. Your unique PRISM perspective for your uniquely distinctive success is just over the horizon. I'm elated with your progress and excited for your continued discoveries to your next level success.

Chapter 7:

Connected to Source, An Indispensable Resource

I am fearfully and wonderfully made.
– Psalm 139:14 NIV

As we proceed within The Diamond Advantage framework, our next domain for consideration is the Spiritual dimension, which consists of mindfulness, gratitude practices, and spiritual awareness and is collectively essential to keeping balance and undue stress in the other domains in support of individual core values. We are indeed expert multi-taskers with responsibilities that pull us in a number of different directions, from taking care of children, caring for parents, work and home responsibilities, and quality time with spouses, as well as with friends and family. These demands, without connection to a Higher Source to guide, direct, protect, and nurture our moral compass, lead to feelings of uncertainty, disarray, and anxiousness. Being connected to Source brings a sense of peace and calm, even during ambiguous seasons. Although particular circumstances may be challenging, there is trust and confidence that God, the Universe, Allah, or however you refer to Source, will take care of you. A peace beyond logical understanding is exactly what each of us needs to navigate the varied demands of a high-achieving life.

Mindfulness. Let's start with mindfulness. Putting formal religion aside, mindfulness practices span across doctrines for believers and non-believers, as well as for those practicing and non-practicing religious sects. Mindfulness, by definition, is the practice of looking inward with a consciousness and awareness of present thoughts. It involves accepting thoughts without judgment, or deciphering right or wrong. It allows for keen attention to thoughts, feelings, environment, and sensations. Hundreds of research studies have documented the physical and mental benefits from regularly practicing mindfulness through meditation. It is recommended that we sit in Zen for at least twenty minutes per day, and, if the schedule allows, even longer, just to be alone with our thoughts. It is also recommended that we practice mindfulness before we need it in dire and ultra-stressful situations. Mindfulness' advantages have positive effects for executives and school children alike. In my experience, mindfulness allows dedicated time to connect to Source to rejuvenate clarity, transparency, and accord. It creates space for calmness and cooler heads to prevail, inciting a virtuous cycle that influences us through a refreshed and more grounded lens. I had the gratifying opportunity to attend a leadership conference in October 2016 led by the world-renowned Deepak Chopra. He shared numerous insights that let an indelible impression; however, three shimmer with effervescence.

First, he opened the talk with a Carl Jung quote that encapsulates the underpinning of this domain.

> *He who looks outside, dreams~*
> *He who looks within, awakens.*
> – CARL JUNG

In my view, we need both – to dream *and* to awaken. Dreaming in consciousness allows one to create a vision for the future. It's the catalyst that incites transformational change. Certainly, that vison needs to be acted upon to bring it forth into reality. However, looking within provides clues as to the dreams' unlimited possibilities and unbounded creativity. It begins to softly create a new reality with perception and emotion. The inward awakening serves as a guided light gently providing direction – a lamp at your feet in some regard.

Secondly, Chopra assuredly shared, "Stretch more than you can reach, and be 'SMART' about it. Connect to mission, then build structure." In essence, dream big, make a plan to get there, and align with core values and strengths. This ideal fundamentally aligns with the core principles of The Diamond Advantage framework. This construct enables the ability to be intentional and purposeful about how to posture to power forward. It makes room to be present and attuned to inherent frequencies and preferences within.

And finally, Chopra's sage advice centered on synchronicity. Specifically, "Unconsciousness or consciousness; things work together due to the undeniable harmony in the universe." Said another way, for Christians, like myself, it translates to "All things work together for the good for those the love the Lord (Romans 8:28 NIV)." Through this concept of synchronicity, even challenging experiences and situations should be perceived as occurring within a wholeness system designed to teach a lesson that should be applied to enrich. If we are wonderfully and fearfully created from our Source, through tenderness things aren't happening *to* us, but *for* us – the good, bad, and even the ugly. To become extraordinary, we become better managers of energy – not time. Energy, as alluded to, manifests in four dimensions: physical, emotional, mental, and spiritual. There's a fluidity within each of the fields and it flows between fields. Stated previously, energy flows where attention goes. Because of universal balance and harmony, the success paradigm is energized due to the interest and consideration. The pinnacle of this story is pivoting inward will provide not only insight, but liberate serenity while doing so.

To refresh our senses and being, let's meditate for five minutes. Do you have five minutes? If no, then you precisely need this. Let's get really comfortable in a quiet place while in a sitting position. Close your eyes and be attentive to your breath, breathing in and out, getting more relaxed with each breath. Think about what's stressing you, the deadlines, presentations, reports, etc. Actually see the images in your mind. Continue to breathe. Get rid of those images and think about happy times, perhaps in your childhood, where you are laughing, playing, enjoying yourself. See the detail of those times with the sun on your face, sand in your toes, and even hear the creak of the swing as it whisks you up higher in the air. Now, clear your mind and just be, exist, breathing, in silence. How do you feel in that moment of being? What are you sensing? That's it, we're done. The goal is that this brief meditation resulted in a refreshed feeling, resetting your awareness and energy. Jot down how this Diamond Meditation made you feel. You have the authority to pause at any given time and engage inward. Is this something you can commit to daily, even for short durations? If already in practice, how can Diamond Meditation be integrated into everyday routines?

Gratitude Practices. The more gratitude practices are caused, the more abundance returns effects. Gratitude, for The Diamond Advantage purposes, is not centered on the material. The material gifts will likely be present when living an abundant life, but are ancillary. Our gratitude savors in the impenetrable, inner peace, sound mind, family, a tribe that genuinely cares about your well-being, health, joy, and love.

I am eternally grateful for the divine hand on my life~
that shepherds me
from circumstance to circumstance.
– DR. HEATHER SIMONE

A position of gratitude, even when it's difficult, opens a heart space to receive abundance. This notion, backed by research conducted by the Nature Science Report, showed that metabolic changes occur through forgiveness (a close cousin of gratitude). Due to the emotional connections to our immune system, a one-week retreat had the ability to influence genome behavior. This experiment resulted in self-regulation mechanisms up to seventeen times over homeostasis – literally opening heart space. In full transparency, this is not always an easy task, it's a conscious decision. The decision to be grateful for the lessons the Universe is teaching takes strength and will. In reflection, our experiences are made of a series of decisions. My fervent gratitude is grounded in the understanding that others who have traveled a similar path, attended similar schools, and had similar experiences have not had the outcomes that I've been gifted. Our journeys are unique and there are gifts designed especially for you – with only your name on them. Gifts that will help bolster you to your next level of success. Turning inward through mindfulness and an attitude of gratitude will serve as a guiding light even on the darkest day. All too often our triumphs over pain become drivers for purpose. Embrace the challenge, this success challenge in particular, and get conceptually ready for the diamond life brilliance that lies on the other side. Take a few moments to list five to ten things you are grateful for. It could be an experience, a person, an opportunity, or simply just the ability to be there for another person. How can you integrate this Diamond Gratitude Attitude into daily routines? During a quiet time in the course of your day – early in the morning or later at night works for most – can you acknowledge five to ten things you were grateful for that day? It could be the simplest gesture or feeling that you find appreciation in. Sometimes even sending a quick text to the person that made the difference has profound impressions on your own heart space. Let me be the first to begin: I appreciate you for trusting me to take this success journey with you. I don't take this experience for granted and look forward not only to celebrating with you, but also to supporting you in paying it forward.

Spiritual Awareness. Spiritual awareness is the ability to intimately know oneself and getting to know more of you. It's the ability to be aware of the internal guiding light that some refer to as intuition, to steer our decision making. When spiritually aware, you can discern unspoken communication in interactions because often what isn't said has just as compelling a meaning as what is verbalized. Comparable to other attributes, there is a level of maturity as spiritual keenness is refined. We are spiritual beings at the core and those who leverage inner perceptions have an advantage over those who don't. The situation doesn't change ("the what") but how you handle and react to instances ("the how") is impacted for the better. When professional and personal occurrences are approached from a frame of a positive mindset, where positive intent is the default, it minimizes much of the negative rhetoric that circles in our thinking – calories that could be spent on advancing your Diamond Advantage. Tony Robbins was once asked how he would describe happiness in one word. His response: "Progress."

Progress in becoming more of yourself as you leverage given gifts and talents; progress to become more deliberate in how we spend our time making an impact and living purposefully. There's no shame in the desire to progress and not wanting to settle. Growth is part of the natural order of progression in nature. Further, when you're at the point where you have to consistently dim your light to give others the opportunity to shine, it's time to change your station. Maslow's 1943 *"A Theory of Human Motivation,"* widely accepted research, depicts the existence of universal human needs as illustrated below.

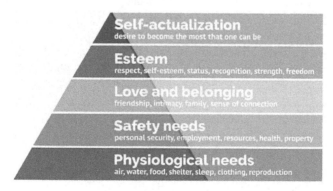

"Maslow's Hierarchy of Needs."
Simply Psychology.

Maslow identified the universal human needs as physiological needs, safety, love and belonging, esteem, and self-actualization; with each building on the prior level in the hierarchy as each level is realized. Self-actualization, at the peak of the hierarchy, is innate to the human development cycle of needs.

For me, my self-actualization as a Christian is grounded in becoming more of a Proverbs 31 woman. Believers and non-believers, I invite you to stay with me as I share my brief interpretation of being a Proverbs 31 woman. In the table below, I address Proverbs 31:10-31 in the NLT, New Living Translation.

Text	Interpretation
10 Who can find a virtuous and capable wife? She is more precious than rubies.	Virtue – We are precious and worthwhile. Be virtuous and capable.
11 Her husband can trust her, and she will greatly enrich his life.	Faithfulness – Speak the truth and earn the trust of others. Be faithful and enrich not only our lives, but others as well.
12 She brings him good, not harm, all the days of her life.	Goodness – Be good to your significant other and family. Cherish and love them.
13 She finds wool and flax and busily spins it.	Hardworking – Be hard workers, never lazy and always improving ourselves.

14 She is like a merchant's ship, bringing her food from afar.	Provider – Provide for your family.
15 She gets up before dawn to prepare breakfast for her household and plan the day's work for her servant girls.	Early Riser – Wake up early and prepare for the day. Be purposeful with our time.
16 She goes to inspect a field and buys it; with her earnings she plants a vineyard.	Business Savvy – (whether working in the home or outside of the home) Pay attention to our world and take advantage of opportunities. Invest earnings in real estate and other dividend-rewarding businesses.
17 She is energetic and strong, a hard worker.	Strength – Be energetic and strong physically, mentally, and spiritually with optimism.
18 She makes sure her dealings are profitable; her lamp burns late into the night.	Endurance – Be hardworking and ensure our dealings are well-handled. Endure even during challenging times.
19 Her hands are busy spinning thread, her fingers twisting fiber.	Well Rounded – Be well rounded and understanding of many skills. Learn and grow different skills.
20 She extends a helping hand to the poor and opens her arms to the needy.	Charitable – Help the less fortunate; love our neighbors and those in need by welcoming them and not judging others.

21 She has no fear of winter for her household, for everyone has warm clothes.	Provide and Trust – Provide for our families, to keep them safe and loved. Trust in the universal plan even during difficult times.
22 She makes her own bedspreads. She dresses in fine linen and purple gowns.	Appropriately Dressed – Not be consumed by our looks, but be appropriately dressed. Treat ourselves like our worth. We are worthy of self-love.
23 Her husband is well-known at the city gates, where he sits with the other civic leaders.	A Good Partner – A marriage or significant relationship is a partnership to include like principles that complement one another.
24 She makes belted linen garments and sashes to sell to the merchants.	Working – Provide for ourselves and family.
25 She is clothed with strength and dignity, and she laughs without fear of the future.	Honorable – Fear nothing but God. Be honorable and strong and carry ourselves as graceful women. Laugh – be happy and optimistic.
26 When she speaks, her words are wise, and she gives instructions with kindness.	Wise – Think before we speak and to do so with kindness. Be wise with our words.
27 She carefully watches everything in her household and suffers nothing from laziness.	Active – Laziness is not an option.
28 Her children stand and bless her. Her husband praises her:	Praise Worthy – We will be rewarded for our hard work.

29 "There are many virtuous and capable women in the world, but you surpass them all!"	Excels – With God in our hearts, we can achieve anything we set our sights on. We will succeed and excel.
30 Charm is deceptive, and beauty does not last; but a woman who fears the lord will be greatly praised.	God Fearing – Fear only your Creator. Live in a way that honors God.
31 Reward her for all she has done. Let her deeds publicly declare her praise.	Rewarded – We will be rewarded for our hard work and dedication. God promises to recognize our faith.

Adapted from "Becoming a Proverbs 31 Woman." Nora Conrad.[71]

Proverbs 31 provides a detailed guide in how we can tap into Source, regardless of whether we're married or not married, or whether we currently have a family of not. It increases our spiritual maturity, which ultimately positively impacts the other areas of our lives – a mindset that promotes inner peace and clarity. Every now and again you come across someone who is glowing on the inside, with a luminosity that can be noticed from the outside. Their life may not be easy, but they glide over the dim moments with relative serenity. The poised approach typically becomes integral to intuitiveness, where the approach to challenges both large and small assumes a certain decorum in perspective. This posture spares energy, not expending loosely on fret and fear. The Proverbs 31 guide, I agree, is extensive and a constant work in progress. We know that striving for progress over perfection is key. If I could sum it up into one affirmation, it would be:

> *She is clothed with strength and dignity~*
> *and she laughs without fear of the future.*
>
> – **Proverbs 31:25**

Chapter 8:

Earned MPS, Master Professional Studies

Be the kind
that makes others
want to up their game.
#PowerPlays
— Dr. Heather Simone

The Master in Professional Studies degree, or MPS, is uniquely geared toward learners who want a more specific skillset to directly apply to their careers. Traditional master's degrees tend to focus more on theory and research. This applied focus is apropos to the immersed experience of the Diamond Success journey. This fifth and final domain of The Diamond Advantage is the Master Professional dimension. We are well on our way to promoting ourselves to a life of significance and have made tremendous progress. This discussion will center on the attributes that more closely align with our desired professional security. While we acknowledge that promotion is important, no consent is granted to achieve next level success at the expense of foregoing other areas of your life. The demand for the MPS certification is, in fact, on the rise. The past two decades touted exponential growth in the number of graduate level degrees awarded – and this trend shows no signs of stopping, according to the 2015 report "Understanding the Changing Market for Professional Master's Programs"[72] by the Education Advisory Board (EAB). According to the report, the demand for the next decade forecasts that graduate degrees will account for nearly one-third of all postsecondary degrees, however not from traditional graduate programs. "The new growth will come primarily from professional master's programs focused on specific job skills that help students gain a new job or advance in an existing position," the EAB report said, referring to degrees like the MPS.

Clearly, we now have an appreciation that professional success is integrated with personal success; therefore, decision making in any given domain of your life should have consideration of the influences to the other areas. This Master Professional domain intricately interlaces with the other domains of The Diamond Advantage framework. Through the signature PRISM perspective, our success journey thus far has created a unique construct through a remarkable passage that: 1) assessed core values and strengths in the personal domain, 2) realized the importance of inter-relational co-creation relationships in the relationships domain, 3) enhanced intellectual curiosity through preferred joyous activities in the intellectual domain, and 4) utilized mindfulness and gratitude to leverage the Source within the spiritual domain. This Master Professional domain will harness all the acquired insights in the preceding domains to bring us just adjacent to diamond life success.

The beauty of this domain is that it provides opportunity for your gifts and talents, your genius zone, to be monetized. Compensation is one of the main drivers of wanting to get to the next level of success, but we now know that aligning to core values and strengths to live a purposeful life proceeds the revenue. Financial achievement was likely part of our original motivation for driving next level success, but in the instances when it doesn't align collectively with our current prioritized values, adjustments should be made to refine *how* this goal is achieved. The income, although re-sequenced, will follow – rest assured. Much of our journey thus far dealt with the relationship we have with ourselves.

In this domain, we pivot to take the learnings we've acquired thus far in this framework and apply them to our interactions with others through leadership. Leadership, regardless of industry, genre, or station, facilitates disruption of the status quo, ushering in room to up-level success, however you define it.

> *Success ~*
> *The accomplishment*
> *of an aim or purpose.*
> – GOOGLE

Success, therefore, is very personalized and tailored to you, based on your specific aim or purpose. A novel notion, purpose-driven success. The first step is to define what success means to you based on the tradeoffs you're willing to make. The output of this Diamond Success journey will be a customized definition of success and a strategic plan of action to implement. The difference between those who are successful and those who are not is action. The successful candidly do the things most others are afraid to do. By now, your success definition may have taken a detour in the success journey. Or perhaps you were on the scenic route and now have a clearer path forward. Either way, you are in a good place because transformation is transpiring. We will delve deeper into your Diamond Success definition in the next chapter, for now we have become familiar with the transience of success.

The Leadership Walk

There is a general belief that diversity is good for business as we transition further into one global society. The forming, storming, norming, and performing[73] cycle in building team effectiveness perhaps takes longer in diverse teams as varying perspectives emerge. Disruptive innovation[74] resulting in a product of the diversity of thought and approach is foundational for organizational longevity through the introduction of a new set of values. From an alternate angle, when diversity is absent, innovation is stalled, thereby limiting the sustainability of an organization to thrive in a global market. Brands such as Kodak, Blockbuster, and Blackberry illustrate a failure to consistently refine offerings and approach through innovative strategies proved to be a detriment. Diversity is reasoned as core to sustaining organizational strategy to compete and thrive in a global market.

Leaders of an organization or departmental team often shape the organization's culture.[75] The change agent in some regards can be substituted for a leader when describing the core responsibility of the transformative leader position. As such, the leader has the responsibility to influence change; further, it has been found that sharing values or common vision employs greater effectiveness in that dynamic.[76] Researchers have demonstrated that participative or consultative leadership is a meaningful form of leadership behavior;[77]therefore, it behooves the leader to create an environment of inclusivity where the leader and follower mutually inform and influence one another. Since the premiere leadership model has evolved to a relational context where the leader and follower influence one another in a shared leadership paradigm it can be viewed as a shared leadership principle or co-creation.[78] How then, as society moves toward a globally diverse society, does the leader remain authentic while influencing and being influenced by others? The concept may perhaps be a common blind spot or challenge for many leaders adding to the complexity of the diverse team dimension.

Leadership consists of personal dominance, interpersonal influence, and relational dialogue,[79] whereas transformational leadership consists of the partnership or shared vision between leader and follower.[80] This paradigm creates the parameters for trust to be incited by the relationship, thereby increasing knowledge share, and ultimately leadership co-creation. Bandura[81] acknowledged that vicarious experiences influence self-efficacy in leadership. Similarly, in the reflected best self (RBS) model[82] micro-changes were employed through socially embedded interactions. Collectively, the research implies that the individual lens, or perspective, frames discrete interpretations and understanding. Based on this comprehensive research, relational dialogue,[83] vicarious experiences,[84] and socially embedded interactions[85] align with the perspective that leadership is relational.

If leadership is created from and within reactions[86] and has elements from a social identity construct that has much to do with internal regulation and control[87] then cultural, gender, and generational optics will inform perspective. This analysis demonstrates that the leader-follower partnership emerges as a platform for co-creation as each constituent is gaining from the co-dependence, a dynamic that emanates both internal and external relational transfers. This notion would suggest a shared knowledge principle positioning where all leadership is shared leadership.[88] This relational interplay can be deemed effective or ineffective[89] because each has a unique framework. The ideal is mainly based on past experiences[90] and cultural dimension[91] that inform individual frames of reference; therefore, exemplary or transformative leadership comprises of having consideration for a constituent's perspective. The concept referred to as the narrow ridge[92] in dialogue – where one holds one's perspective while simultaneously being open to others' views – is the premier leadership approach. In other words, it's important to have a view but equally important to be open to other ideas that may influence your thinking. Not being so rigid in perspective fosters a continuous progression forward. Therein lies the conundrum, or benefit, when cultural differences are integral to the relation.

Counting Your Coins Pays Dividends

My godmother, Aunt Blossom, affectionately called Goddie, taught me my very first and most profound lesson in finances that has stayed with me all the days of my life. She taught me from a very early age the importance of not only saving, but investing my finances. She was my "Rich Dad, Poor Dad" all in one. She stood at about five feet two inches tall with a beautiful caramel color complexion, bronze highlighted hair, and red lipstick to match her fiery no-nonsense demeanor. My godmother loved to cook, and every New Year's Day holiday she would have a celebratory dinner at her home to usher in the new year. Her feasts were enough to feed the multitude! I looked forward to every New Year's holiday knowing that I would be spending the time with her in her two-family Brooklyn home, where she hosted with great delight. The festivities were always jubilant as the classic Bob Marley Caribbean music played in the background, the delicious aroma of authentic spices filled the air, and a handful of people would be dancing in the living room, while others reminisced about old times, laughing and chatting. Every time the doorbell rang, which was quite often, the white fluffy dog could be heard barking in some distant room. As a child, I was fascinated with Goddie's Christmas tree. Sure, it had decorations, but my Goddie also put the Christmas cards she received on the tree. I don't remember what kind of decorations she had, but I always remembered the tree filled with cards from top to bottom. "How on earth did she get so many Christmas cards?" I thought. I stood mesmerized in a daze, taking in all the faces of the fancy cards, some with glitter in stunning holiday colors, and others elaborate nativity scenes. It created a spectacle as the glow of the varying color Christmas lights peeked randomly under the carefully-positioned cards, each telling its own story cradled between the twinkling lights. I was an intrigued spectator, coiffed with shiny black shoes, folded socks with fufu on the hem, a plaid holiday dress, and pigtails with ribbons in my hair. And yes, still to this day, my favorite color besides pink is glitter. I still like fufu, and am matchy-matchy, in a more mature way, but nonetheless the same at the core. My elongated trance was broken by my mother calling me over for dinner. I skipped over and carefully plopped on the couch, making sure I sat on my fufu dress because I didn't want the plastic cover on the couch sticking to the back of my legs.

Anyway, my Goddie gave me a savings bond as a gift for every birthday, Christmas gift, etc. At first,

I really didn't understand the significance and wasn't too pleased to get an envelope that I just handed over to my mother at each birthday. By the time I went to college, I seemed to have enough for at least a full card deck in varying amounts. I was astonished when Mom cashed them in to pay for my first wedding during my sophomore year in college. That caught my attention and I have never had the same attitude toward finances since! I immediately started buying bonds for my son, but by then that market waned and the lackluster returns were disappointing. Rest assured, the tacit lesson from my tribe was already taught. Goddie was a single mother landlord that taught me to invest early, even if only a little amount. This was my crucible that has stayed with me for a lifetime. Yes, I love shoes *and* purses but I'm disciplined to pay myself first (and then buy the shoes after I get paid). With a corporate job and automatic banking, I honestly didn't know when pay day was. The funds were swept out of my daily expense account to a separate account. All I knew was what I had to spend for the week; and when that allotted amount was exhausted, we didn't eat out, but stayed within the budget, period.

Don't buy shoes~
Buy buildings.
– NELY GALÁN

Financial Fabulousness

Diamond Financial fabulousness is being astute about cash flow and passive income streams. Warren Buffet recommends having at least seven streams of income. It doesn't take a math whiz to understand that entrepreneurship and real estate investments should be in that seven-stream portfolio of investments. I'll save the details for the graduate level for those seeking the #DiamondLife, but simply put, each income strategy should have a positive cash flow and invest the realized gains. By no means should this constitute investment advice, but fundamental financial literacy is vital for you to have the ability to achieve uber radiance. In today's digital age, we have the opportunity to be creative with diversified income streams. The gamut is limited only to your imagination; for example: investment pools, art work, real estate investment trusts or REITS, and online retail stores, as well as service-oriented establishments. There is a distinct differential in financial savvy between men and women, with the financial behavior exhibited by men exceeding that of the women in nearly every category. The trending numbers are alarming! The average person works approximate forty years of their life, twenty-something to sixty-something. I personally have targets that are in decade blocks to materially up-level *at least* every ten years, which are then backed into five- and three-year aims; essentially incrementally progressing toward the Diamond Ten-year Blocks. However, the insight from current trends denotes a shift in perspective.

The trends are as follows:

- Research indicates that our life expectancy has been extended with a forecasted 35% of the population above age 65 by the year 2030, versus 22% in 2018. This means that the need to stay in the workforce beyond 40 years, potentially up to 50 years, would likely be in order to be financially prepared to adequately manage resources for our extended life expectancy, even while health care costs are on the rise.

- This expansion would mean that individuals ages 85 years and older would increase from 5.8 million in 2010 to 8.7 million by the year 2030.

- Between the years 2010 and 2050, the United States population ages 65 years and older will nearly double; the population of ages 80 and older will nearly triple; and the number of nonagenarians and centenarians (individuals in their 90s and 100s) will in fact quadruple.

- The disparity between women's and men's retirement plans is staggering. According to 2016 census data, women still earn reportedly 80% less than their male counterparts and have

30% less retirement savings on average than men. Men start earlier, save more aggressively in percentage and vehicle selection, and spend less time away from the workforce.

The core Diamond Financial Strategies that help to solve for the financial disparity between men and women include guidelines for a solution: 1) pay yourself first, 2) save 10% into a retirement vehicle, 3) invest based on cash flow analysis (manage debt), and 4) increase the number of streams of (passive) income. Retire like a boss. If your goal is to improve financial strategies, even small progressive steps will have residual gains. Start where you have interests. For example, when my son had his first job, all he wanted was to buy the latest sneakers with his pay. After a few chats, he quickly learned to pay himself first and we opened him his own online savings account. Then we took it another step and discussed investing in individual stocks. I had him research the companies he was interested in, which included the well-known amusement park in Florida, the sneakers with a swoosh, and the company that makes his cell phone. Even one stock purchase in each of these organizations would benefit from long-term gains based on earnings and compounded dividends. How are you progressing based on the four-part Diamond Financial

Strategy? How would you rate your progress in each financial section on a scale of one to five?

Diamond Brand Strategies

Organizations tout brand strategies as an essential element to thrive in a global marketplace. As such, we as individuals should also be invigorated about brand strategy efforts. Your brand incudes all aspects associated with you as an individual, from executive presence, online presence, the way in which you communicate, emotional intelligence, and performance record. All of these aspects are integral to one's brand. To manage your brand equity, certainly ensure that acquired competencies are continuously cultivated and new competencies are being acquired. Ensure that authenticity is the substance that permits your effervescence to luminate, and consistency is upheld at all times. Every exchange either adds to, or subtracts from, your brand equity. You are the winning edge.

> *Your brand is like your reputation,*
> *Your most important asset.*
> – RICHARD BRANSON

I recall working with Abigail, a young professional that wanted to get promoted from her analyst role to the manager level. She and I had numerous coaching conversations to create a plan that she could implement. Abi was eager to put strategy into action. As we discussed her personal brand and what she wanted to emulate, I realized that Abi was getting in her own way. She spoke of her peers' Ivy League education and majors in econ and finance that could not compare to her marketing degree. I listened without interruption as she explained her rationale. Because her formal training was different, she felt junior to her colleagues. These negatives self-talks showed up in everything she did. Abi certainly had a different approach to problem solving and solutioning when compared to her associates, but her belief that thinking differently and having alternate perspectives was unconstructive is undoubtedly incorrect. I encouraged Abi to share her viewpoints more often and speak up when she had insight to enrich the conversation. We added this attribute to her brand strategy to ultimately augment her value proposition. Abi worked on getting comfortable with being uncomfortable, the exact spark needed to incite growth. Her leaders and peers took notice of the change in her willingness to share ideas and contribute, even when her suggestions were not applied to that very solution. She began to be invited to more meetings because her perceived value proposition was elevated. Abi did eventually earn a promotion, but to this day she credits her brand equity as the differentiating factor.

Clarity on brand strategy is central for positioning perceived value proposition. It is in our direct control to modify it to increase competitive advantage. While a resume synthesizes past performance and professional experiences, a brand strategy consists of a forward-looking outlook. It tells a story that brings value. The Diamond Brand Strategy consists of your mission statement, unique value proposition, competencies acquired and desired, as well as desired target markets and partnerships. The below table is the Diamond Brand Strategy template that you can use to capture how you wish to augment your brand equity. As a special gift, a completed Brand Strategy template is located on my website, populated and completed for your reference. Cheers!

MISSION STATEMENT

VALUE PROPOSITION

COMPETENCIES (*DESIRED)

(e.g. Management and Performance), (e.g. Technical Expertise), (e.g. Customer Service), (e.g. Team Development)

(e.g. Management and Performance)	(e.g. Technical Expertise)	(e.g. Customer Service)	(e.g. Team Development)

TARGET MARKET(S)

Geographic Area	Industry Types	Size of Organization	Culture

TARGET PARTNERSHIPS/ORGANIZATIONS

(e.g. Service Providers)	(e.g. Start-Up Equipment Provider)	(e.g. Private IT Staff)	(e.g. Network Consulting)

To conclude this final domain of The Diamond Advantage framework, take some time to complete your Brand Strategy. Take as much time as you need on this activity. Be thoughtful, your future depends on it! Your brand strategy is a reflection of your intensified radiance. Dare to illuminate without limitation.

If content is king~
Then marketing is queen
And She runs the household.
— ADAPTED FROM GARY VAYNERCHUCK

Chapter 9:

A Luminous Decision Abounds

When first things are put first,
Second things are not suppressed,
But increased.
— C.S. LEWIS

So, they eliminated my job? Right, that's what I was told. I left the c-site office inspired and encouraged to start fresh. As promised, calls poured in inquiring about exploratory conversations for future roles within the organization. They were just that – exploratory. Pleasantries of needing to get requisitions approved and opened became circular in follow-ups that didn't materialize. As the days turned to weeks, disappointment set in. Not at any one moment did I ever question why

– at least, not this time around. I'd already been through that self-deprecating drill the first time around – when I departed from my prior role. When you know your worth, there's no need to wait for validation from others. A decision, indeed, needed to be made.

The Good, Bad, Ugly, and Alternatives

Because I'm not only an advocate for the Diamond Life Strategies, it's my way of life. What showed its rearing head was the opportunity to put beliefs into action. The Diamond Decision Making is a three-part process, with a bonus. This entails: 1) The Good, Bad, Ugly, and Alternatives, 2) Risk and Reward, 3) Diamond Baseline Check, and a Bonus. Resisting instinct and introspectively applying the decision construct was the best action I could take, considering emotions are often indiscriminate. I shared this strategy time and again with protégés, clients, and associates needing a structure to the best possible outcome when making a decision. However, this was incredibly challenging, and no easy task to heed your own advice, but I applied the construct because of the tremendous implications this decision would have, not only impacting me but my family. The best thing I knew to do was take action.

The Good. There is always a silver lining in every situation and circumstance. The ability to see the positive is not an unrealistic rose-colored glasses fluke, but a disciplined approach that insightfully acknowledges that experiences are linked to an overall movement – even when it stings! With this perspective in mind, must there be some good in being displaced from your job? Yes, affirmative, there is good in every situation, even the challenging ones. After pensive thought using intellect to search my heart, the glow of my inner compass revealed the answer. I had maxed out on contributing value to my current role and it was time to move on to other responsibilities that permitted me growth and stimulation in alternate interests. The "end" perhaps was truly a beginning – a vacancy where other chosen facets could vacillate without limitation. Further, this unexpected opportunity, catalytic moment, is a chance for promotion to the next level of success, better aligning with the unique Diamond Baseline blueprint. The rational mind, or negative chatter, says otherwise. Chatter characteristically sends diminishing beliefs. Recognize chatter for what it is, simply a noisy distraction trying to derail progressive thoughts. Recognize, don't immobilize. Recognition is the control that keeps the decision prudent and not thoughtless having a head in the clouds. This grounding is not to immobilize where it prevents forward progress due to the incited fear or analysis paralysis. Chatter's place should be held in the same regard as Haters; their place is informational, a mere data point.

The Bad. Oooooo, the bad. Employment is the means by which we all live and survive. Maslow's Hierarchy of Needs avows that safety is the foundation, the first and preliminary need, that all else advents from. This is a loss for the predictable security of personal financial wellness. This uncertainty most certainly will influence the other PRISM domains holistically. The personal, relational, intellectual, and spiritual states all readjust to accommodate for this void. Searching for a new role, the next level of success is a job in itself and it likely will take several months to secure a new position.

The Ugly. The most unpleasant part is that savings resources will now need to be depleted during this time. It's a menacing thought that once the new role is attained, a course correction would be needed to maintain current resource levels. Also, the new establishment, whether within the current organization or otherwise, will call for a reset in developing a proven track record, collaboration, and brand establishment.

The Alternative. Retire early! Not even remotely possible, a wishful dreamy idea but not rational. A plausible alternative is to work for yourself. Become a full-fledged entrepreneur and business owner who makes and breaks your own rules. The upside is unlimited creativity and potential income, the downside is the obvious: inconsistency in income, particularly in the beginning.

Risk, Reward, and the Diamond Baseline. Now. Let's move onto the next part of the decision-making process, Risk and Reward. With every decision there is also an inherent risk. As a guide, usually the higher the risk, the higher the potential reward. Whether preferences are conservative, moderate, or aggressive, targeting suitable balance between the two sides of the spectrum is important. The potential upside is equivalent to the potential downside. The question becomes, how much are you willing to potentially risk to secure your goal? Said another way, what near-term tradeoffs are you willing to make to achieve your longer-term goal of getting to the next level of success? In this case, I was content taking a sizable risk to attain the reward. It was a matter of believing in my own abilities and banking on myself. And finally, validation of the Diamond Baseline needs to occur. Does the next step align with your core values and strengths? Will it allow you to become more *you*? No matter what the decision, compromising brilliance was not an option, not at this juncture.

The Bonus. Every strategic plan should include a bonus, or what I call a contingency. On the slim chance that the original plan falls through or is stalled, there is a back-up in place as a catchall. The aim is that the Bonus won't need to be initiated, but it reduces the downside risk, a layer of protection that also gives peace of mind. So, there you have it, the Diamond Decision Making process – 1) good, bad, ugly, and alternatives, 2) risk and reward, 3) The Diamond Baseline, and the bonus.

What is a girl to do?

After a great deal of reflection, my realization was that I needed to get more comfortable with being uncomfortable – growth. The inner glow became intensified with the messaging that I could do more, have a greater impact, and be a better service without being confined to the traditional 9 to 5. The servant leader with the expertise of years of acquired knowledge and professional and personal experiences wanted to share that to benefit others – to become the transformational leader that allows others to see the authentic power within themselves. The truth is that the authenticity already exists and it's simply a matter of removing the veil to see your diamonds sparkle. For me, this decision essentially taps deeper into my unique differentiator and genius zone, and as an added bonus, I get compensated for it. My passion has always been to help others get to the next level in their professional life, with a sweet spot for women. I've created The Diamond Advantage framework and have applied it in my own life. My own experiences, challenges included, serve as a model for the success structure. At the end of the day, The Diamond Advantage advocates creating a customized strategic plan and taking action to achieve the desired reward. That's it! No fancy formulas or complicated math. Just making a plan for you, taking action, repeating. Over and over again, to your own heart's desire. Plan. Action. Repeat.

My plan to move closer to my Diamond Baseline was to do more of the coaching, mentoring, and developing of others in an official capacity. The action was to formally create the system and program. And the bonus, or contingency, was that I would take another role, a job in a Fortune 100, while I formalized the program. The Universe, however, said no. The numerous obstacles and resistance were counter to an organic flow toward the traditional role. I took heed and poured wholeheartedly into scaling Diamond strategies. This book that you're reading today is one of the outputs of that effort. Living a life of purpose that aligns with one's individual unique Diamond Baseline is the most rewarding and meaningful life of significance, the epitome of newly-defined success. Promote yourself without losing yourself, or the ones you love.

Diamond Fascination and Its Parts

Congratulations for taking this success journey! We have experienced an insightful transformation within the success paradigm. We began with the realization that the tensions resulting from aiming for the desires of both the head and the heart are not a figment of your imagination. The concerns of next level success *and* relationships you care about is not only affirmed, but validated that you were not alone in your struggle. My story is your story; sharing my own personal experiences and coaching cases of others' journeys creates a powerful testament similar to the challenges you may be experiencing in progressing to next level success. There is a customized solution to this conundrum based on the five-dimensional Diamond Advantage PRISM framework that will bring clarity and significance to the personalized decision of next level success. The exploration guided us through the Personal, Relationships, Intellectual, Spiritual, and Master Professional domains with keen insights along the way.

In the Personal domain of the framework, we discussed the need to get connected to your unique core values and strengths, uncovering what matters most. Through personal reflections, core preferences were identified in the first step in the Personal domain of the framework. Our success journey then pivoted to the Relationships domain where we learned about *why* the relationships are so meaningful and the potential loss experienced without those relationships. Relational positioning through an established watermark told of the importance each network has in our lives. This was connected back to Diamond Baseline, an extension of the core values that were uncovered. Then, in the fourth, or Intellectual, domain, we developed an appreciation that intellectual growth was part of the original motivation for driving next level success, but in the instances when it doesn't align collectively with your current prioritized values of the other areas of your life, adjustments should be made to refine *how* this goal is achieved. Exploring personal interests and not being limited to traditional forms of education is vital, learning is everywhere in our current digital age.

In the fifth and final domain, the Master Professional domain, we experienced transformational insight, where the promotion once thought was the desire wasn't the best alignment with your current core values and strengths. Promotion will still certainly be pursued, however with *redefined* success criteria, under new terms. Professional success, integrated with personal success, therefore calls for a comprehensive and prioritized customized plan that extends to the other areas of your life. Planning is an ongoing process that continues to be evaluated along the way. It's a living, breathing document that's not shelved somewhere and dusted off at leisure. It should be reviewed periodically for on-going edits and mitigators as nuances arise. The Diamond Advantage: Plan. Action. Repeat.

Intensifying Your Brilliance

What about you? Are you ready to take the next step to your next level success? You now have the tools to equip yourself to navigate the complexity of additional scope, responsibility, and commitment promotion brings. Through compelling personal stories, leadership research, and insightful exercises, a customized strategy redefines success with purpose, integrity and significance, by integrating professional and personal aims – in essence, having it all. Are you ready to make that decision? I assume you are. It's likely your definition is based on new criteria gleaned from the insights gained from this journey. We've reflected, experienced realizations, and now it's time for the reward. The newly found success definition brings clarity to the strategic success plan. A clear vision will result in clear results. The Diamond Success Declaration is as follows: My strategic plan is to leverage _____ skill(s) in order to _____ by _____ (day, date, and time).

As an example of a Diamond Success Declaration:

My strategic plan is to leverage **my tax accounting** skill(s) in order to **open my own tax consulting business** by **Saturday, January 1st at 5 p.m. EST**.

Or:

My strategic plan is to leverage **my product knowledge and presentation** skill(s) in order to **apply**

for an Internal Wholesaler role by **Saturday, January 1st at 5 p.m. EST**.

This will lead to further developing your revised personal mission statement and value proposition on the Diamond Brand Strategy template. This is an exciting time; you are well on your way to next level success. The Universe needs your expertise and anxiously awaits for your radiance to illuminate unabashedly, giving others the carte blanche to do the same.

Shine bright like a diamond.

— RIHANNA

Chapter 10:

Not All Grandeur and Pomp

Do not go
where the path
may lead~
Go instead
where there is no path
and leave a trail.
– EMERSON

Cut, color, and clarity have been defined. The realization that you can have it all without losing yourself or the relationships you care about by creating a customized plan based on your prioritized values has been crystalized. Through The Diamond Advantage framework we plan, act, and repeat. My dear friend, we know that for even the best of plans and intentions, there will be challenges. I call it grit. According to Google, there are two definitions of grit. The first definition states that grit is small, loose particles of stone or sand; and the second: grit is courage and resolve; strength of character. I want to shout! Going back to the beginning of our success journey, we discussed the disruptive and combustive trek that all diamonds experience to get to their brilliance. Diamonds are essentially made of tightly latticed carbon that, under the right corrosive conditions, forms a beautiful gem. Carbon, within the grit of the earth's mantle, disrupts, eventually forming the diamond. Yet, for each of us to achieve our diamond brilliance we rely on our resolve, or grit, to get through the disruption. Clearly, it is not all grandeur and pomp and circumstance.

Winners Don't Win by Chance

As you may have noticed by now, I continually seek inspiration through affirmation, quotes, and visualizations. Being well aware of "Chatter," this is my proactive way to keep my fire lit. Hearing others' stories of triumph firsthand, in particular, has a way of inciting new flickering into my glow. I had the fortunate chance to attend a talk led by Steven Bradbury, a four-time short track speed skating Olympian.

As the story goes, the headlines globally went viral when he won the 1,000-meter event at the 2002 Winter Olympic games in Salt Lake City. Steven was the underdog going into this race as the eighth best in the world for his event at that time. With the help of his coach, his strategy going into the race was to stay out of the way of the other four contestants and perhaps one or two might fall, allowing the rest of the heat an opportunity to medal. He was the oldest in his field at the time and this particular race would be his fourth for the night. He agreed to the strategy and, to even his own surprise, all four of the other contenders got entangled, permitting him to cruise into the gold victory. Globally there were mixed feelings as to *how* he won the gold. Steven remained humble immediately at the Medal Ceremony and to this day. He never claimed to be the best and shared that luck was on his side. I have a very different perspective. Winners don't win by chance. Winners create luck, their opportunity to further shine their radiance is manifested through hard work, determination, and the intuitive alliance with their personal North Star. This was his fourth Olympic game, coming back from a leg injury that required over one hundred stitches, in addition to subsequently breaking his neck at the C4 vertebrae. He trained six days a week for a minimum of five hours a day. Luck? No, my friend. Steven was so dedicated to rewriting the definition of winning and getting to the next level success. He had grit through every challenge he faced and in the end was rewarded for it. Winners don't win by chance, but through relentlessly pursuing goals through plan, action, and repeat.

Steven's story is just one that made the headlines. There are numerous conquests, like Bonnie St. John, who became the first African-American ever to win medals in Winter Olympic Paralympic competition. She, too, sent glimmers of what's possible in my psyche as I observed firsthand her recounting the additional difficulties she needed to overcome based on her gender and skin color. Her sport was already hard enough, considering her right leg was amputated at age five. She, too, displayed an extraordinary amount of grit as she planned, took action, and repeated as necessary, raising money when her mother could no longer afford to send her to training. Wow, how she sparkles.

The Grit Equation

It's well established that grit is a necessary element to achievement, but how do you get grit? Let's go back to your why, the fundamental reason for motivation. Your why tells of the reason for being and drive. Getting reacquainted with your why serves as fuel that ignites your flame. This is your legacy building at its finest.

When they can't remember what you said,
they will always remember how you made them feel.
– Maya Angelou

Yes, the journey is not for the faint of heart, and takes hard work and determination, but it also takes guidance and reliance on the experts. Like Steven, for example, he became the best based on the expert guidance of his coach. A coach is an accountability partner who is there with you every step of the way. Clearly, his plan to win was extremely personalized based on his strengths, targeted goal, and the current external factors of the environment. I highly recommend engaging with a coach for your success journey.

Give Back and Pay Forward

This success journey is whatever you make of it. If you believe you can change the world, you can. This is a community of practice as more join this Diamond Advantage Movement. I applaud you for your great effort and celebrate your new success with you. I want to hear from you as you share new success. We are relational and success begets additional success. I ask one thing, that you give back and pay forward the insights that have transformed you and have made a difference in your success. Use your influence to makes a difference for someone else. Let's legacy build together. Join a board, coach, advocate for others' success and most of all, let your life be representative of your successful #Diamond Life.

Very truly yours,

Heather

A cut above ~
Take a closer look at me there's more than meets the eye
The radiance within me glows from many years gone by.
But I'm an "A CUT ABOVE" and beyond can compare
I have facets, a girdle, a pavilion, and a crown
I'm an "A CUT ABOVE" and I'm world renown
– ADAPTED FROM JUDI KIPNER WOLF[93]

Blank Brand Strategy Template

Insert quote optional

Photo Optional

HEATHER SIMONE
123 My Way Drive
(555)123-4567
Email: HEATHERSIMONE123@GMAIL.COM
LinkedIn:

Logo Optional

MISSION STATEMENT

VALUE PROPOSITION

COMPETENCIES

(e.g. Management and Performance)	(e.g. Technical Expertise)	(e.g. Customer Service)	(e.g. Team Development)
•	•	•	•

TARGET MARKET(S)

Geographic Area	Industry Types	Size of Organization	Culture
•	•	•	•

TARGET PARTNERSHIPS/ORGANIZATIONS

(e.g. Service Providers)	(e.g. Start-Up Equipment Provider)	(e.g. Private IT staff)	(e.g. Network Consulting)
•	•	•	•

The Diamond Advantage Professional Marketing Plan - HeatherSimone.com

Completed Brand Strategy Template

"She believed she could, so she did."

HEATHER SIMONE, DBA
123 My Way Drive
(555)123-4567
EMAIL: HEATHERSIMONE123@GMAIL.COM
LINKEDIN: WWW.LINKEDIN.COM/IN/HEATHER-BROWN-DBA-PMP

MISSION STATEMENT
Award winning corporate executive and leadership authority resolved to influence next level success for professional women

VALUE PROPOSITION
An experienced senior leader in managing strategic initiatives with in-depth experience in investment and financial services at Fortune 100 companies managing the sales, operations, and risk tolerances of various multi-million dollar teams/accounts. Exemplary leadership in managing initiatives which benefit the enterprise that aligns with the strategic vision of the firm. Performance demonstrates expertise in developing people, managing process, and simplifying complex change. Collective professional experiences positions to be uniquely qualified to influence next level success for professional women.

COMPETENCIES

Leadership & Mgmt. Performance	Technical Expertise	Client Service Delivery	Team Development
• Lead cross-functional change to achieve targets • Strategic planner that minimizes risk while maximizing reward • Action oriented to consistently exceed expectations	• Synthesis & analysis of data to identify trends • Develop and utilize KPI metrics to determine targets and needed pivots • Streamline process to maximize outcomes	• Under promise and over deliver to make "sticky" • Create wow! experience for Clients through ease of doing business –"Only you" • Set expectations and update accordingly increasing customer loyalty	• Coach and develop teams to sustained breakthrough performance • Founded corporate mentoring program • Model community leader providing biz development training

TARGET MARKET(S)

Geographic Area	Industry Types	Size of Organization	Culture
• Global audience	• Individual intrapreneurs & entrepreneurs	• Start-ups to Fortune 100	• Willing to be coached & take action

The Diamond Advantage Professional Marketing Plan – HeatherSimone.com

Completed Brand Strategy Template

TARGET PARTNERSHIPS/ORGANIZATIONS

Service Providers	Scale Digital Footprint	Affiliates	Network Consulting
• Digital Marketing • PR Representatives • Brand Marketers	• Podcasts • Guest Speaker radio / TV/ talks • Articles	• Professional Business Leaders • Church organizations • Authors	• Speaking engagements • Corporate Organizations • Educational Institutions and Affinity Groups

The success journey for each of us~

is unique as a precious diamond that forms over time ~

through stimulating, yet disruptive environments~

that ultimately radiates a brilliance that luminates unprecedented excellence.

—Dr. Heather Simone.

The Diamond Advantage Professional Marketing Plan - HeatherSimone.com

Acknowledgements

I'm forever thankful for the Divine hand on my life that's guided me from circumstance to circumstance, teaching me life's gems that will last a lifetime. I thank Almighty God for placing this project in my heart; it was only through His will that this became a reality. I am eternally grateful for His grace and mercy. My heart is full!

To my beloved mother, Ena, for the endless sacrifices you made so that I can shine brilliantly. You instilled in me a belief of "what's possible." There is no earthly amount that adequately recognizes your efforts. I can only dream to have the same impact with my own children. I dedicate this work to you. My success is because of you. Love you with all my heart!

To my Dad, Leslie, who passed down my business sense and relentless work ethic. I thank you. I must have heard it a million times, "You're just like your father!" Yes sir, I am! Love you Dad!

To my two sons, Devonté and Demetri, who inspire me to shine brighter every day. You both are the source of my drive and determination. To my son Devonté, who shared, "Mom, I have so much respect and am truly inspired by you." To my son Demetri, who repeatedly said, "Mom, you've been sitting at that desk for days." The collective inquiries became the underpinning of my drive to completion. My biggest desire is to have modeled my life to something you both can be proud of and are inspired by. Love you to pieces!

To my husband, Dan, affectionately known as "Twin," your enduring love and partnership preceded my brilliance. I'm forever grateful for your unwavering support of every "big idea" of mind. From the bottom of my heart, thank you for taking this journey with me. Love you beyond measure!

To my brothers and sisters, slew of cousins, and long line of powerful aunties. Thank you all for showing me what perseverance looks like. I could not have done this work without my tribe, my family. Mother, Mama, Aunts, and Sisters, I am thankful for all the strong women in my life. I am because you were. I stand on the shoulders of strong women who made something out of nothing.

To my coaches, mentors, and sponsors, who are unapologetically in my corner, but who also tell me the truth even when it's not what I want to hear. Thank you for guiding me through challenges big and small. The learning and insight I've gained through lived experiences ignited the spark to pay it forward to others.

To the Morgan James Publishing team: Special thanks to David Hancock, CEO & Founder for believing in me and my message. To my Author Relations Manager, Tiffany Gibson, thanks for making the process seamless and easy. Many more thanks to everyone else, but especially Jim Howard, Bethany Marshall, and Nickcole Watkins.

To my church family, led by the remarkable Rev. Dr. Soaries and First Lady Soaries, thank you for your expert guidance in keeping me spiritually grounded while strengthening my Christian walk.

Last and certainly not least, thank you to the women who strive for next level success. Your tenacity, resolve, and fortitude creates a multiplier effect that's shifting the paradigm. Power forward, my friend!

Thank you for the opportunity to be an inspiration and empower others in their quest for next level success. Promote yourself without losing yourself on your terms. Here's to the diamond life!

#Blessed

#Diamond Life

#Have It All

Thank You!

Dear friend,

First and foremost I want to thank you for trusting me to take this success journey with you!

You are primed with the insight and tools needed to take action. I am excited for what's in store for you. Your plan is just that without action. A plan is not some mere task list that is shelved, dusted off, and revisited now and again. Your customized success plan is your North Star that is reviewed often for reassessment and evaluation based on how you're tracking. You are extraordinarily courageous as you implement your success path and drive forward to your next level brilliance. Consistency in action is key as you are accountable for your outcomes. Be honest with yourself as you review your progress in 30, 60, 90 days, and beyond. Don't be afraid to make adjustments along the way, as long as collectively you're moving towards your goal.

I'm here for you! I would love to hear about your progress as well as work through any challenges you may face in your journey. I look forward to unpacking your challenges, getting to the heart of the issue, so that you can realize your true radiance on the other side of the horizon. My passion is coaching and developing others to achieve professional and personal accomplishments and I would welcome for us to connect in a strategy session to better understand how I can support your needs. I work with rising stars, young professionals, as well as well-established executives and entrepreneurs. My approach is both individual, with one-on-one coaching, as well as group coaching depending on the need. In addition, training sessions at your organization are available. Let's connect!

Let's connect for a strategic session or to join the Diamond Advantage community. There is strength in numbers so networking and engaging with like-minded individuals can only be beneficial. It's a movement; let's #PowerForward together!

Shine brilliantly,

Heather

#DiamondAdvantage
HeatherSimone.com
Heather@HeatherSimone.com

About the Author

Dr. Heather Simone is the founder and CEO of the award-winning firm The Diamond Advantage LLC. She is uniquely qualified to lead transformative strategic leadership sessions within The Diamond Advantage organization due to her  extensive corporate career with over fifteen years as a Fortune 100 Financial Services executive.

Dr. Heather earned her Bachelor of Science degree in Biological Sciences from Rutgers University and her MBA with an interest in International Finance from Rider University. She holds over seven licenses within the financial services industry, including the Series 7. Most recently, Heather pursued her Doctor of Business

Administration in Leadership from Capella University. Her research analyzed the impact of transformational leadership within diverse teams to identify attributes that optimize team performance.

Dr. Heather is a highly sought panelist and international speaker. Most notably, she has spoken at the Money, Wealth and Business Conference in South Africa and lectured at both Rutgers and Rider Universities and numerous Fortune 100 conferences.

Dr. Heather is an exemplary community leader with passion in working with women, millennials, and high-potential professionals. Through the LIFE 360 program she has developed strategies for young professionals to exceed in leadership, innovation, faith, and overall excellence. She has received numerous awards for her accomplishments and is also a board member of JC Community Health Center, advocating for women's health issues.

A first-generation American of Jamaica, West Indies descent and a mother of a US Army soldier, she currently resides in New Jersey with her husband and two sons.

HeatherSimone.com
Heather@HeatherSimone.com

References

1   "Diamond Fun Facts." Gemological Institute of America. https://www.gia.edu/gia-news-research-diamond-fun-facts.

2   "Brilliant (diamond Cut)." Wikipedia. August 24, 2018. https://en.wikipedia.org/wiki/Brilliant_(diamond_cut).

3   "Do Diamond Inclusions Affect Diamonds Brilliance?" Home What Makes Rubies Such a Valuable Gem Comments. https://www.briangavindiamonds.com/news/diamond-inclusions-affect-diamonds-brilliance/.

4   Slaughter, Anne-Marie. "Why Women Still Can't Have It All." The Atlantic. June 20, 2018. https://www.theatlantic.com/magazine/archive/2012/07/why-women-still-cant-have-it-all/309020/.

5   Sandberg, Sheryl, and Nell Scovell. Lean In:
        Women, Work, and the Will to Lead. New York:
        Alfred A. Knopf, 2017.

6   Krawcheck, Sallie. "10 Ways to Improve Your
        Company's Diversity Results." LinkedIn.
        January 08, 2014. https://www.linkedin.
        com/pulse/20140108113954-174077701-10-
        ways-to-improve-your-company-s-diversity-
        results?trk=mp-reader-card.

7   Always Brand. "Always #LikeAGirl." YouTube.
        June 26, 2014. https://www.youtube.com/
        watch?v=XjJQBjWYDTs.

8   "The Clever Strategy Obama's Women
        Staffers Came up with to Make Sure They
        Were Being Heard." The New York Times.
        September 14, 2016. http://nytlive.nytimes.
        com/womenintheworld/2016/09/14/the-clever-
        strategy-obamas-women-staffers-came-up-with-
        to-make-sure-they-were-being-heard/.

9   Boris Groysberg and Katherine Connolly. "Great
        Leaders Who Make the Mix Work." Harvard
        Business Review. October 27, 2014. https://hbr.
        org/2013/09/great-leaders-who-make-the-mix-
        work.

10   "A Shocking Fact about Diamond Clarity They
        Don't Want You to Know." The Diamond Pro.
        https://www.diamonds.pro/education/clarity/.

11   Robson, Steve. "Absolute Perfection: World's Largest 'flawless' Diamond Could Sell for More than $20million." Daily Mail Online. March 13, 2013. http://www.dailymail.co.uk/news/article-2292727/Absolute-perfection-Worlds-largest-flawless-diamond-sell-20million.html.

12   "A Shocking Fact about Diamond Clarity They Don't Want You to Know." The Diamond Pro. https://www.diamonds.pro/education/clarity/.

13   Haas, Hartmut. "How Can We Explain Mixed Effects of Diversity on Team Performance? A Review with Emphasis on Context." Equality, Diversity and Inclusion: An International Journal 29, no. 5 (2010): 458-90. doi:10.1108/02610151011052771.

14   Thomas, David A. "Diversity as Strategy." Harvard Business Review. August 01, 2014. https://hbr.org/2004/09/diversity-as-strategy.

15   "MLT Partner Spotlight: How Clorox Is Building a Diverse Talent Pipeline." Management Leadership for Tomorrow. May 19, 2016. https://ml4t.org/blog/mlt-partner-spotlight-how-clorox-is-building-a-diverse-talent-pipeline /.

Hewlett, Sylvia Ann, Melinda Marshall, and Laura Sherbin. "How Diversity Can Drive Innovation." Harvard Business Review. August 01, 2014.

https://hbr.org/2013/12/how-diversity-can-drive-innovation.

16   Hunt, Vivian, Dennis Layton, and Sara Prince. "Why Diversity Matters." McKinsey & Company. https://www.mckinsey.com/business-functions/organization/our-insights/why-diversity-matters.

17   Fan, Donald. "Proof That Diversity Drives Innovation." DiversityInc. July 30, 2018. http://www.diversityinc.com/diversity-management/proof-that-diversity-drives-innovation/.

18   Hunt, Vivian, Dennis Layton, and Sara Prince. "Why Diversity Matters." McKinsey & Company. https://www.mckinsey.com/business-functions/organization/our-insights/why-diversity-matters.

19   Maznevski, M., and DiStefano, J. "Foundations of cross-cultural management." SAGE. https://www.mckinsey.com/business-functions/organization/our-insights/why-diversity-matters. 2008.

20   "The business of inclusion." Microsoft Store. https://www.microsoft.com/en-us/diversity/business-of-inclusion/default.aspx. 2016.

21   Adapted from "Live Your Core Values: 10 Minute Exercise to Increase Your Success." Root Cause Analysis System, Training and

Software by TapRooT®. http://www.taproot.com/archives/37771.

22   Clifton, Donald. "Discover Your Clifton Strengths." 2017.

23   Wallis, Nancy C., Francis J. Yammarino, and Ann Feyerherm. "Individualized Leadership: A Qualitative Study of Senior Executive Leaders." The Leadership Quarterly 22, no. 1 (2011): 182-206. doi:10.1016/j.leaqua.2010.12.015.

24   Nayar, Vineet. "Recasting the Role of the CEO: Transferring the Responsibility for Change-How Leaders Can Tap the Creative Energy of Employees." In Employees First, Customers Second: Turning Conventional Management Upside down. Boston, MA: Harvard Business Press, 2010.

25   Ackoff, R. "Systems Thinking and Thinking Systems." System Dynamics Review 10, no. 2/3 (1994): 175-88. doi:10.1002/sdr.4260100206.

26   Smith, Wendy K., and Marianne W. Lewis. "Toward A Theory of Paradox: A Dynamic Equilibrium Model of Organizing." Academy of Management Review 36, no. 2 (2011): 381-403. doi:10.5465/amr.2011.59330958.

27   Smith, Wendy K., and Marianne W. Lewis. "Toward A Theory of Paradox: A Dynamic Equilibrium Model of Organizing." Academy of

Management Review 36, no. 2 (2011): 381-403. doi:10.5465/amr.2011.59330958.

28   Smith, Wendy K., and Marianne W. Lewis. "Toward A Theory of Paradox: A Dynamic Equilibrium Model of Organizing." Academy of Management Review 36, no. 2 (2011): 381-403. doi:10.5465/amr.2011.59330958.

29   Park, Chinta Lee, M. Lee, J. Turner, and L. Kilbourne. "Macro Fit versus Micro Fit of the Organization with Its Environment: Implications for Strategic Leadership." International Journal of Management 28.2 (2011): 488-92.

30   Clifton, Donald. "Discover Your Clifton Strengths." 2017.

31   Moore, Amanda, and Ketevan Mamiseishvili. "Examining the Relationship Between Emotional Intelligence and Group Cohesion." Journal of Education for Business 87, no. 5 (2012): 296-302. doi:10.1080/08832323.2011.623197.

32   Wheatley, M.J. Leadership and the New Science: Discovering Order in a Chaotic World. San Francisco, CA: Berrett-Koehler Publishers., 2012.

33   Wheatley, M.J. Leadership and the New Science: Discovering Order in a Chaotic World. San Francisco, CA: Berrett-Koehler Publishers., 2012.

34   Wheatley, M.J. Leadership and the New Science: Discovering Order in a Chaotic World. San Francisco, CA: Berrett-Koehler Publishers., 2012.

35   Wheatley, M.J. Leadership and the New Science: Discovering Order in a Chaotic World. San Francisco, CA: Berrett-Koehler Publishers., 2012.

36   Seagal, Sandra and David Horne. "Human Dynamics for the 21st Century." The Systems Thinker. 2003. https://thesystemsthinker.com/human-dynamics-for-the-21st-century/.

37   Seagal, Sandra and David Horne. "Human Dynamics for the 21st Century." The Systems Thinker. 2003. https://thesystemsthinker.com/human-dynamics-for-the-21st-century/.

38   Seagal, Sandra and David Horne. "Human Dynamics for the 21st Century." The Systems Thinker. 2003. https://thesystemsthinker.com/human-dynamics-for-the-21st-century/.

39   Pearce, W. Barnett, and Kimberly A. Pearce. "Combining Passions and Abilities: Toward Dialogic Virtuosity." Southern Communication Journal 65, no. 2-3 (2000): 161-75. doi:10.1080/10417940009373165.

40   Sollisch, Jim. "The Cure for Decision Fatigue." The Wall Street Journal. June 10, 2016. https://

www.wsj.com/articles/the-cure-for-decision-fatigue-1465596928.

Tierney, John. "Do You Suffer from Decision Fatigue?" The New York Times. August 17, 2011. https://www.nytimes.com/2011/08/21/magazine/do-you-suffer-from-decision-fatigue.html.

Black, Sierra. "Decision Fatigue: Why Willpower Isn't Always Enough." Forbes. September 19, 2011. https://www.forbes.com/sites/moneybuilder/2011/09/02/decision-fatigue-why-willpower-isnt-always-enough/3/#570857912bbe.

41   "Why Chronic Stress Messes with Your Health." The Huffington Post. November 07, 2013. https://www.huffingtonpost.com/2013/11/07/chronic-stress-health-inflammation-genes_n_4226420.html.

42   "Sallie Krawcheck." MM.LaFleur. https://mmlafleur.com/most-remarkable-women/sallie-krawcheck.

43   Huffington, Arianna. Instagram, June 15, 2018, https://www.instagram.com/p/BkC3yuPHTLN/?hl=en&taken-by=ariannahuff.

44   Nayar, Vineet. "Recasting the Role of the CEO: Transferring the Responsibility for Change-How Leaders Can Tap the Creative Energy of Employees." In Employees First, Customers

Second: Turning Conventional Management Upside down. Boston, MA: Harvard Business Press, 2010.

45   Park, Chinta Lee, M. Lee, J. Turner, and L. Kilbourne. "Macro Fit versus Micro Fit of the Organization with Its Environment: Implications for Strategic Leadership." International Journal of Management 28.2 (2011): 488-92.

46   Pearce, C.L. "The Future of Leadership: Combining Vertical and Shared Leadership to Transform Knowledge Work." Academy of Management Executive 18, no. 1 (2004): 47-57. doi:10.5465/AME.2004.12690298.

47   Nayar, Vineet. "Recasting the Role of the CEO: Transferring the Responsibility for Change-How Leaders Can Tap the Creative Energy of Employees." In Employees First, Customers Second: Turning Conventional Management Upside down. Boston, MA: Harvard Business Press, 2010.

48   Richardson, Kurt A., and Michael R. Lissack. "On the Status of Boundaries, Both Natural and Organizational: A Complex Systems Perspective." Emergence 3, no. 4 (2001): 32-49. doi:10.1207/s15327000em0304_3.

49   Goodwin, V.L., J.L. Whittington, B. Murray, and T. Nichols. "Moderator or Mediator? Examining

the Role of Trust in the Transformational Leadership Paradigm." Journal of Managerial Issues 23, no. 4 (2011): 409-25. http://www. pittstate.edu/business/journal-of-managerial-issues/index.dot.

50   Goodwin, V.L., J.L. Whittington, B. Murray, and T. Nichols. "Moderator or Mediator? Examining the Role of Trust in the Transformational Leadership Paradigm." Journal of Managerial Issues 23, no. 4 (2011): 409-25. http://www. pittstate.edu/business/journal-of-managerial-issues/index.dot.

51   Goodwin, V.L., J.L. Whittington, B. Murray, and T. Nichols. "Moderator or Mediator? Examining the Role of Trust in the Transformational Leadership Paradigm." Journal of Managerial Issues 23, no. 4 (2011): 409-25. http://www. pittstate.edu/business/journal-of-managerial-issues/index.dot.

52   Lauring, Jakob, and Jan Selmer. "Openness to Diversity, Trust and Conflict in Multicultural Organizations." Journal of Management & Organization, 2012, 1870-894. doi:10.5172/ jmo.2012.1870.

53   Goodwin, V.L., J.L. Whittington, B. Murray, and T. Nichols. "Moderator or Mediator? Examining the Role of Trust in the Transformational

Leadership Paradigm." Journal of Managerial Issues 23, no. 4 (2011): 409-25. http://www.pittstate.edu/business/journal-of-managerial-issues/index.dot.

54   Chari, S. "Understanding and Enhancing Decision-making Skills." International Journal of Clinical Leadership 16, no. 4 (2008): 163-66.

55   Richardson, Kurt A., and Michael R. Lissack. "On the Status of Boundaries, Both Natural and Organizational: A Complex Systems Perspective." Emergence 3, no. 4 (2001): 32-49. doi:10.1207/s15327000em0304_3.

56   Richardson, Kurt A., and Michael R. Lissack. "On the Status of Boundaries, Both Natural and Organizational: A Complex Systems Perspective." Emergence 3, no. 4 (2001): 32-49. doi:10.1207/s15327000em0304_3.

57   Gadman, Sean, and Cary Cooper. "Strategies for Collaborating in an Interdependent Impermanent World." Leadership & Organization Development Journal 26, no. 1 (2005): 23-34. doi:10.1108/01437730510575561.

58   Heracleous, Loizos. "Boundaries in the Study of Organization." Human Relations 57, no. 1 (2004): 95-103. doi:10.1177/0018726704042716.

59   Moliterno, Thomas P., and Douglas M. Mahony. "Network Theory of Organization: A Multilevel

Approach." Journal of Management 37, no. 2 (2010): 443-67. doi:10.1177/0149206310371692.

60 Moliterno, Thomas P., and Douglas M. Mahony. "Network Theory of Organization: A Multilevel Approach." Journal of Management 37, no. 2 (2010): 443-67. doi:10.1177/0149206310371692.

61 Nayar, Vineet. "Recasting the Role of the CEO: Transferring the Responsibility for Change-How Leaders Can Tap the Creative Energy of Employees." In Employees First, Customers Second: Turning Conventional Management Upside down. Boston, MA: Harvard Business Press, 2010.

62 Park, Chinta Lee, M. Lee, J. Turner, and L. Kilbourne. "Macro Fit versus Micro Fit of the Organization with Its Environment: Implications for Strategic Leadership." International Journal of Management 28.2 (2011): 488-92.

63 Merle, Andrew. "The Reading Habits of Ultra-Successful People." The Huffington Post. December 07, 2017. https://www.huffingtonpost.com/andrew-merle/the-reading-habits-of-ult_b_9688130.html.

64 "Timeline of the Introduction of Color Television in Countries." Wikipedia. August 24, 2018. https://en.wikipedia.org/wiki/Timeline_of_the_introduction_of_color_television_in_countries.

65   Merle, Andrew. "The Reading Habits of Ultra-Successful People." The Huffington Post. December 07, 2017. https://www.huffingtonpost.com/andrew-merle/the-reading-habits-of-ult_b_9688130.html.

66   Wheatley, M.J. Leadership and the New Science: Discovering Order in a Chaotic World. San Francisco, CA: Berrett-Koehler Publishers., 2012.

67   Wheatley, M.J. Leadership and the New Science: Discovering Order in a Chaotic World. San Francisco, CA: Berrett-Koehler Publishers., 2012.

68   Kim, W. C., & Mauborgne, R. A. (2004). Value innovation. *Harvard Business Review, 82*(7/8), 172-180. https://hbr.org/.

Kim, W. C., & Mauborgne, R. A. (2005). Blue ocean strategy: From theory to practice. *California Management Review, 47*(3), 105- 12. doi:10.2307/41166308.

69   Clear, James. "How Long It Really Takes to Form A Habit, According to Science." The Huffington Post. June 10, 2014. https://www.huffingtonpost.com/james-clear/forming-new-habits_b_5104807.html.

70   Gladwell, Malcolm. Outliers. Harmondsworth: Penguin, 2009.

71   Conrad, Nora. "Becoming a Proverbs 31
      Woman." https://www.noraconrad.com/blog/
      becoming-a- proverbs-31-woman.

72   "Understanding the Changing Market for
      Professional Master's Programs." Education
      Advisory Board. https://www.eab.com/
      research-and-insights/academic-affairs-forum/
      studies/2015/understanding-the-changing-
      landscape-for-professional-masters-programs.

73   Tuckman, Bruce W. "Developmental Sequence in
      Small Groups." Psychological Bulletin 63, no. 6
      (1965): 384-99. doi:10.1037/h0022100.

74   Bower, Joseph L. and Clayton M. Christensen.
      "Disruptive Technologies: Catching the Wave."
      Harvard Business Review. April 16, 2018.
      https://hbr.org/1995/01/disruptive-technologies-
      catching-the-wave.

75   Tsui, Anne S., Zhi-Xue Zhang, Hui Wang,
      Katherine R. Xin, and Joshua B. Wu. "Unpacking
      the Relationship between CEO Leadership
      Behavior and Organizational Culture." The
      Leadership Quarterly 17, no. 2 (2006): 113-37.
      doi:10.1016/j.leaqua.2005.12.001.

76   Tsui, Anne S., Zhi-Xue Zhang, Hui Wang,
      Katherine R. Xin, and Joshua B. Wu. "Unpacking
      the Relationship between CEO Leadership
      Behavior and Organizational Culture." The

Leadership Quarterly 17, no. 2 (2006): 113-37.
doi:10.1016/j.leaqua.2005.12.001.

77 Yukl, Gary, Angela Gordon, and Tom Taber.
"A Hierarchical Taxonomy of Leadership
Behavior: Integrating a Half Century of
Behavior Research." Journal of Leadership &
Organizational Studies9, no. 1 (2002): 15-32.
doi:10.1177/107179190200900102.

78 Drath, Wilfred H. The Deep Blue Sea: Rethinking
the Source of Leadership. San Francisco, Calif:
Jossey-Bass, 2001.

79 Drath, Wilfred H. The Deep Blue Sea: Rethinking
the Source of Leadership. San Francisco, Calif:
Jossey-Bass, 2001.

80 Bass, Bernard M. Leadership and Performance
beyond Expectations. New York, Ny: Free Press,
1985.

81 Bandura, Albert. "Self-efficacy: Toward a
Unifying Theory of Behavioral Change."
Psychological Review 84, no. 2 (1977): 191-215.
doi:10.1037/0033-295x.84.2.191.

82 Roberts, Laura Morgan, Jane E. Dutton, Gretchen
M. Spreitzer, Emily D. Heaphy, and Robert E.
Quinn. "Composing the Reflected Best-Self
Portrait: Building Pathways for Becoming
Extraordinary in Work Organizations." Academy

of Management Review 30, no. 4 (2005): 712-36. doi:10.5465/amr.2005.18378874.

83   Drath, Wilfred H. The Deep Blue Sea: Rethinking the Source of Leadership. San Francisco, Calif: Jossey-Bass, 2001.

84   Bandura, Albert. "Self-efficacy: Toward a Unifying Theory of Behavioral Change." Psychological Review 84, no. 2 (1977): 191-215. doi:10.1037/0033-295x.84.2.191.

85   Roberts, Laura Morgan, Jane E. Dutton, Gretchen M. Spreitzer, Emily D. Heaphy, and Robert E. Quinn. "Composing the Reflected Best-Self Portrait: Building Pathways for Becoming Extraordinary in Work Organizations." Academy of Management Review 30, no. 4 (2005): 712-36. doi:10.5465/amr.2005.18378874.

86   Berger, Charles R. "Interpersonal Communication: Theoretical Perspectives, Future Prospects." January 10, 2006. https://onlinelibrary.wiley.com/doi/abs/10.1111/j.1460-2466.2005.tb02680.x.

87   Carroll, Brigid, and Lester Levy. "Leadership Development as Identity Construction." Management Communication Quarterly 24, no. 2 (2010): 211-31. doi:10.1177/0893318909358725.

88   Drath, Wilfred H. The Deep Blue Sea: Rethinking
      the Source of Leadership. San Francisco, Calif:
      Jossey-Bass, 2001.

89   Marrs, P.C. The Enactment of Fear in
      Conversations-gone-bad at Work. PhD diss.,
      2007. ProQuest Dissertations & Theses Global.

90   Roberts, Laura Morgan, Jane E. Dutton, Gretchen
      M. Spreitzer, Emily D. Heaphy, and Robert E.
      Quinn. "Composing the Reflected Best-Self
      Portrait: Building Pathways For Becoming
      Extraordinary In Work Organizations." Academy
      of Management Review 30, no. 4 (2005): 712-36.
      doi:10.5465/amr.2005.18378874.

91   Bing, John W. "Hofstedes Consequences:
      The Impact of His Work on Consulting and
      Business Practices." Academy of Management
      Perspectives 18, no. 1 (2004): 80-87.
      doi:10.5465/ame.2004.12689609.

92   Pearce, W. Barnett, and Kimberly A. Pearce.
      "Combining Passions and Abilities: Toward
      Dialogic Virtuosity." Southern Communication
      Journal 65, no. 2-3 (2000): 161-75.
      doi:10.1080/10417940009373165.

93   Adapted from Wolf, Judi Kipner. "Judi Kipner
      Wolf." Whiteflash. October 11, 2012. https://
      www.whiteflash.com/about-diamonds/diamond-
      education/what-are-diamonds-made-of-1295.htm.